MODERN IDEAS IN CHESS

BY

RICHARD RÉTI

Translated by John Hart

DOVER PUBLICATIONS, INC.
NEW YORK

Published in Canada by General Publishing Company, Ltd., 30 Lesmill Road, Don Mills, Toronto, Ontario.

Published in the United Kingdom by Constable and Company, Ltd., 10 Orange Street, London WC 2.

This Dover edition, first published in 1960, is an unabridged and unaltered republication of the second edition published by G. Bell & Sons in 1943.

Standard Book Number: 486-20638-6

Manufactured in the United States of America
Dover Publications, Inc.
180 Varick Street
New York, N. Y. 10014

FOREWORD

A REISSUE of this, the most important contribution to the literature of chess since Tarrasch's "300 Games of Chess", has long been wanting. Here Richard Réti has concentrated the essence of the modern view of the game, and so great has been the success of his ideas that no expert will be found so foolish nowadays as to quarrel with his conclusions. I well remember what a revelation the book was to me when I read it as a boy—what new horizons and fresh ways of thought on the game were disclosed to me. It seemed that everything that had been static and wooden in chess, suddenly, at the touch of this magician's wand, became dynamic and vital. In "Modern Ideas in Chess" Réti had created at once the manifesto of what was then a revolutionary chess movement, and an entrancingly lucid study of the methods of the great masters.

A few words with regard to the life of the author are necessary. He was born at Pezzinok, near Pressburg in Czechoslovakia, on May 28th, 1889; studied mathematics at Vienna University, and whilst there realised that his true bent was chess. It was in Vienna that he met and became fast friends with another great writer on the game, Dr. Savielly Tartakower, and it was against the latter that he then played the charming off-hand game which, as typifying the poetic qualities of Réti's chess genius, is here reproduced.

Opening—Caro-Kann defence. *White* R. Réti. *Black* Dr. S. Tartakower. (1) P—K 4, P—Q B 3. (2) P—Q 4, P—Q 4. (3) Kt– Q B 3, P×P. (4) Kt×P, Kt—B 3. (5) Q—Q 3, P—K 4. (6) P×P, Q—R 4 ch. (7) B—Q 2, Q×K P. (8) Castles, Kt×Kt. (9) Q—Q 8 ch! K×Q. (10) B—Kt 5 Dbl. Ch. K—B 2. (11) B—Q 8 Ch-mate.

From 1907 onwards he took part regularly in international chess tournaments. In these his chief successes were 1st prize at Kaschau 1918, Budapest 1918, Rotterdam 1919, Amsterdam 1920 and Vienna 1920; second prizes

in the important tourneys at Mährisch-Ostrau 1923 and
Vienna 1923, and—most notable of all—the winning of
first prize in that landmark in modern tournaments, Gothen-
burg 1920. Historically, his most outstanding achievement
in the post-war years was his crushing defeat of the then
world champion, Capablanca at New York 1924 at a time
when the latter seemed invincible.

Though not devoid of success in the next few years, on
the whole his performances in international chess were dis-
appointingly inequal. Nevertheless the chess world regarded
this as a purely temporary phase and it was a sad shock
of surprise to us all to hear of his death from scarlet fever
at a Prague hospital on June 6th, 1929. He was therefore
just forty when he died.

The above summary does not include all Réti's varied
activities in chess. During his lifetime he held the record
for blindfold simultaneous play, having played 21 blindfold
games simultaneously at Sao Paulo in Brazil. As a composer of endgame studies he ranked with the greatest, being
especially distinguished by the subtle charm of his King
and Pawn endgames.

Apropos of this there is related an anecdote typical of
the man. In the closing stages of an international tournament he was playing one of the weaker competitors and
had obtained a won game. It was his turn to move—an
obvious one since all he had to do was to protect a threatened
piece. He seemed to fall into a brown study, did not move
for ten minutes; then suddenly started up from his chair—
still without making his move—and sought out a friend
who was present in the congress rooms. To him he explained
that he had just conceived an original and entrancing idea
for an endgame study. Not without difficulty his friend
dissuaded Réti from demonstrating and elaborating this
idea on his pocket chess set, and Réti returned, somewhat
disgruntled, to the tournament room, made some hasty
casual moves and soon lost the game.

Without troubling at all about this loss, Réti at once
returned to his hotel and spent almost the whole of the
night in working out his endgame study. As a consequence

he lost his next game through sheer fatigue and with it went his chances of first prize. He perfected a beautiful endgame composition at considerable financial loss.

It was this pursuit of the ideal that robbed Réti of many successes in practice and to this one may ascribe his lack of great triumphs in the tournament world during the last few years of his life. During this period the paradox was presented of his fame as a theoretician ever increasing as his practical successes diminished. His researches in opening theory have left an indelible mark on modern technique. Réti's opening, a dangerous weapon in the hands of a master, is now in current use and productive of much more lively and ingenious chess than the outworn gambits of antiquity.

To return to the present book, the reader will be interested to learn of the somewhat fortuitous nature of its genesis. In the early 1920's Réti published a series of articles in chess magazines, partly as a manifesto of the new school, but chiefly to blast the pretensions of one, Franz Gutmayer, who, to quote Réti, "might perhaps in fifty years' time be so advanced as to comprehend Steinitz and has at present achieved this much at least—a partial understanding of Morphy". Gutmayer, a prolific writer of books claiming to show the reader the way to chess mastery, is now quite forgotten, or, at most, exists like a fly preserved in amber in the first edition of Réti's book.

From the later edition, however, Réti expunged topical controversial matter, remodelling the book into its present harmonious whole.

A harmonious eloquence is indeed a characteristic and recurring feature of this book. The writer was fortunate enough to have a subject exactly fitting to his powers. Whether he is describing with poetic fervour the charm of Schlechter's style, depicting the metallic brilliance of Capablanca's technique, explaining how masterly combinations are conceived over the chess board or tracing the history of succeeding schools of chess, Réti's faculty of fixing the reader's interest is unsurpassed.

H. Golombek.

December 1942.

AUTHOR'S PREFACE

IF we compare the games of chess of recent years with the older ones, we shall find, even with a superficial consideration of the games handed down to us from olden times, absolutely different openings and unusual contours of positions. New ideas rule the game and have considerable similarity with the ideas of modern art. As art has turned aside from naturalism, so the ideal of the modern chess master is no longer what was called "sound play" or development in accordance with nature. That is to say in accordance with nature in the most literal sense; for that old kind of development was directly copied from nature.

We believe to-day that in the execution of human ideas deeper possibilities lie hidden than in the works of nature: or to put it more accurately, that at least for mankind the human mind is of all things the greatest that nature has provided. We are, therefore, not willing to imitate nature and want to imbue our own ideas with actuality. Those pioneers in art, who are difficult to understand, are acknowledged by the few and jeered at by the many: Chess is a domain in which criticism has not so much influence as in art; for in the domain of chess the results of games decide, ultimately and finally. On that account "Modern Ideas in Chess" will perhaps be of interest for a more extended circle. The artists who, in spite of derision and enmities, follow their own ideas, instead of imitating nature, may in times of doubt, from which no creative man is free, know, and cherish hope therefrom, that in the narrow domain of chess these new ideas in a struggle with the old ones are proving victorious.

I have in this volume attempted to indicate the road along which chess has travelled; from the classicism of Anderssen, by way of the naturalism of the Steinitz school, to the individualistic ideas of the most modern masters.

CONTENTS

MODERN IDEAS IN CHESS

CHAPTER I

THE DEVELOPMENT OF POSITIONAL PLAY

I. COMBINATION

WE perceive after a careful consideration of the evolution of the chess mind that such evolution has gone on, in general, in a way quite similar to that in which it goes on with the individual chess player, only with the latter more rapidly.

The earliest books on the game as played to-day go back no further than to the commencement of modern times. They are written by masters of that period, and, from the beautiful combinations contained in them, we recognise, quite distinctly, the chess talent of the particular authors. But on the whole they were gróping in the dark, for the gross and glaring errors that occur in those works lead us to the conclusion that to obtain an accurate grasp of a position, or " sight " of the board, meant as much trouble to the experienced player of that time as it does to the beginner of to-day.

A chess player in his early stages, who for the first time plays over the games of those masters, experiences unbounded delight in the combinations to be found in them, more especially those involving sacrifices. The other parts of the game seem to have but little interest for him. On those lines was chess played until the middle of the nineteenth century, practically until Morphy appeared upon the scene.* During that period, quite at the beginning of the game a player tried to work out combinations quickly, with the conviction that they were much the most valuable factors in the game.

The chess hero of that epoch, with whose name, for most players, is associated the first grasp of the limitless beauties of our game, was Adolph Anderssen (1818–1878). One of his most beautiful and best known combinations is the following :—

Diagram I.

White : Anderssen.   Black : Dufresne.

---

*An exception was the great Chess Philosopher, A. D. Philidor (died 1795), who was too much in advance of his time to be properly understood.

Anderssen, quite undisturbed by the threat of his opponent against his King's position, plays a deeply considered preparatory move—

1. Q R—Q 1

Dufresne accepted the " gift from the Greeks " without any foreboding.

1.	....	Q × Kt
2.	R × Kt ch	Kt × R
3.	Q × P ch	K × Q
4.	B—B 5 ch	K—K 1

(If 4 .... K—B 3, mate follows by 5 B—Q 7).

5 B—Q 7 ch, and mate follows next move with B × Kt. Still prettier would the ending have been had Black played 2...K—Q 1 instead of 2...Kt × R. We should then have had 3 R × P ch, K—B 1; 4 R—Q 8 ch! A surprising turn in events. The rook can be taken in three different ways—

4.	....	Kt × R

If 4 ...... R × R then 5 P × Q
If 4 ...... K × R then 5 B—K 2 ch wins Black's Queen.

5.	Q—Q 7 ch	K × Q
6.	B—B 5 ch	and mate next move.

If we ask ourselves what there is in this particular combination or, for a matter of that, in any combination, that compels our admiration, the reply will be that in the game just quoted it is the quiet inconspicuous introductory move (1 R—Q 1) which just by reason of its inconspicuousness operates with such great charm. A strong and more strikingly attacking move could have been made without any regard as to what was to follow. But it is the choice by Anderssen of the less obvious move, whose meaning only becomes clear later on, that forces us to the appreciation of the deep working of his brain.

It is the same with a sacrifice. A combination composed of a sacrifice has a more immediate effect upon the person playing over the game in which it occurs than another combination, because the apparent senselessness of the sacrifice is a convincing proof of the design of the player offering it. Hence it comes that the risk of material, and the victory of the weaker material over the stronger material, gives the impression of a symbol of the mastery of mind over matter.

Now we see wherein lies the pleasure to be derived from a chess combination. It lies in the feeling that a human mind is behind the game dominating the inanimate pieces with which the game is carried on, and giving them the breath of life. We may regard it as an intellectual delight, equal to that afforded us by the knowledge that behind so many apparently disconnected and seemingly chance happenings in the physical world lies the one great ruling spirit—the law of Nature.

2. POSITIONAL PLAY

The layman thinks that the superiority of the chess master lies in his ability to think out 3 or 4, or even 10 or 20, moves ahead. Those chess lovers who ask me how many moves I usually calculate in advance, when making a combination, are always astonished when I reply, quite truthfully," as a rule not a single one." Formerly, in Anderssen's time, the ability to make combinations was in fact the very essence of chess talent. Since then, however, the chess mind has further developed, and the power of accurately calculating moves in advance has no greater place in chess than, perhaps, skilful calculation has in mathematics.

Applying a simple mathematical formula we shall easily see how impossible, and on the other hand how objectless, it would be in general to try to work out in advance exact sequences of moves. Let us consider a position in which there is no distinct threat : an ordinary tranquil position. We shall certainly not be going too far if we assume that each side has every time on an average three feasible moves ; that being the number to be taken into account, generally speaking, in order to effect the calculation. If I want to work out, now, all the variations on the basis of one full move (*i.e.*, one move by me and one by my opponent) for all the variations, I should have to consider already $3^2 = 9$ different variations. On the basis of two full moves the number of possible variations already amounts to $3^4 = 81$ their computation being at the most possible in correspondence games.

Should we further wish to calculate the number of variations of 3 moves of Black and White respectively we find that the number of such variations is represented by $3^6 = 729$: in practice therefore scarcely possible of execution. Allowing we took the trouble to make the above calculations what would be the advantage to be derived therefrom ? The computation of the variations would only have some sense if, from the resulting respective positions, we could in the end discover which combination would be the most favourable. We cannot assume, again in a tranquil position, that after 3 moves so thought out, a clear result will be evident. Therefore from the point of view of the ordinary player, who thinks that in chess nothing counts but combinations, a further calculation is called for ; and it is clear with what rapidity, exceeding that of all human calculation, the number of possibilities would increase after a few moves.

Combinations in chess can only be made when the number of the possibilities to be reckoned in advance is a limited one, that is to say when the moves of one player force the opponent to make moves already foreseen. This can happen either if a move contains a certain threat which can be parried by the opponent only in one way or at any rate only in a very few ways : for example if an opponent's piece is exchanged, so that he in reply must take a piece, or again if check be called. A combination by one player involves therefore forced moves by the opponent. It is only in such cases that it is possible to calculate much in advance, as many as twenty—perhaps more—moves, because the number of the different variations is still very small.

Speaking generally the essential object of this work is to deal not with exact combinations but with all kinds of considerations relating to the development and evolution of the strategic mind and which dictate moves in chess. The method of playing chess by which we do not try to work out single moves in advance is known as positional play. Play by means of combinations and positional play are not opposed to each other, but rather mutually supporting. The scheme of a game is played on positional lines, the decision of it is, as a rule, effected by combinations. This is how Lasker's pronouncement that positional play is the preparation for combinations is to be understood.

3. PAUL MORPHY

Paul Morphy, the American, had in his early years a most brilliant chess career. After having gained in 1857, when only twenty years old, his first prize in the master tournament in New York he beat the greatest European masters, and finally Anderssen, in a decisive manner. To the question : What was the secret of that success ? the reply is that he had a wonderful talent for combinations. Anderssen possessed that talent no less than Morphy and in addition more imagination than the latter. The deciding advantage in Morphy's favour was the fact that he was the first positional player.

Positional play in early days was nearly always governed by general principles. Morphy, it is true, had written nothing himself ; but his games clearly contained the basic principles for the treatment of open positions. Morphy was not at home in close positions, and in these often not fully a match for some of his contemporaries. The games lost by Morphy were mostly those that partook of a close character.

The most important principle in the treatment of opening positions to be learnt from Morphy's games, is that which subsequently became to all chess lovers a matter of course : the one which lays down that in the opening, with every move development is to be advanced.

As an example I give the normal position in the Evans Gambit which is arrived at after the following moves :—

1.	P—K 4	P—K 4
2.	Kt—K B 3	Kt—Q B 3
3.	B—B 4	B—B 4
4.	P—Q Kt 4	B × P
5.	P—B 3	B—R 4
6.	P—Q 4	P × P
7.	Castles	P—Q 3
8.	P × P	B—Kt 3

Diagram II.

Before Morphy's time, as the principle of development was not yet known, if a player had no opportunity for a combination he made either an attacking or a defensive move. Therefore, in the position in Diagram II, either 9 P—Q 5 or 9 Q—

Kt 3, or even the purely defensive move 9 P—K R 3 would have been the usual continuation. It was first through Morphy's example that what appears to us the most natural developing move, namely 9 Kt—B 3, has become usual.

Another example : A master game of the first half of the nineteenth century opened with the following moves—

1.	P—K 4	P—K 4
2.	Kt—K B 3	Kt—Q B 3
3.	P—Q 4	P × P
4.	B—Q B 4	B—B 4
5.	Kt—Kt 5	....

Diagram III.

Morphy would certainly never have made this move, an attacking one instead of a developing one.

| 5. | .... | Kt—K 4 |

This move looks attractive. It protects the pawn
at K B 2 and at the same time attacks the B at
B 4.

     6.   B × P ch   ....

The combination was as follows—

     6. ....   Kt × B
     7. Kt × Kt   K × Kt
     8. Q—R 5 ch   P—Kt 3
     9. Q × B   ....

White wins a pawn and has a distinct advantage.

An American chess player tried the same combination against Morphy.   In the position shown
in Diagram IV. Morphy did not allow himself to be
inveigled into making the seemingly excellent
move 5...Kt—K 4, for he saw that it had the disadvantage of not developing another piece and
that it ran counter therefore to his own principles.

Diagram IV.

Morphy simply played—

| 5. | .... | Kt—R 3 |

and as White as a sequel to 5 Kt—Kt 5 went on with the combination originally designed, the game proceeded as follows—

6.	B × P ch	Kt × B
7.	Kt × Kt	K × Kt
8.	Q—R 5 ch	P—Kt 3
9.	Q × B	P—Q 3

and the difference showed itself distinctly. The pawn at Q 5 is protected, as Morphy (in consequence of his developing move 5 Kt—R 3) exchanged the otherwise undeveloped piece and not the already developed Kt at Q B 3. White has a bad game and the premature attack by 5 Kt—Kt 5 is refuted.

4.   FOURTH GAME IN THE MATCH—
ANDERSSEN—MORPHY

THIS contest between two different schools shows us clearly that the player who, merely through his imagination and power of combination, gave to the game its particular aspect, was bound to lose in the long run ; because Morphy's positional play and the principle of quick development proved ultimately superior to mere talent, however strong.

White : Anderssen.   Black : Morphy.

1.	P—K 4	P—K 4
2.	Kt—K B 3	Kt—Q B 3
3.	B—Kt 5	P—Q R 3
4.	B—R 4	Kt—B 3
5.	P—Q 3	B—B 4
6.	P—B 3	P—Q Kt 4
7.	B—B 2	....

White had from now onwards a fantastic idea of attack. He wanted to effect a mate at K R 7. To conceive such a plan at that moment is not justified by any weakness in Black's position, and seems, according to our modern views, to be almost ludicrous. But we shall see what dangers Anderssen, in the furtherance of his idea, is able to conjure up against his opponent, and appreciate how he could have succeeded brilliantly against a weaker opponent.

7.	....	P—Q 4
8.	P×P	....

This move only furthers the opponent's development and affords Black more terrain in the centre.

On that account 8 Q—K 2 would have been much better. But Anderssen still wants to make the attack along the diagonal, Q Kt 1—K R 7 and therefore willingly exchanges his K's pawn.

| 8. | .... | Kt × P |
| 9. | P—K R 3 | .... |

A loss of time. But Anderssen must, as a continuation of his plan of attack, soon play P—Q 4 and fears that Black may hinder him by B—Kt 5. Morphy, in contrast to Anderssen, goes quietly on with his development.

| 9. | .... | Castles |
| 10. | Castles | P—R 3 |

This move (contrary to White's P—K R 3) forms part of the development. Morphy wants to play B—Q 3 without being disturbed by White's Kt—Kt 5.

11.	P—Q 4	P × P
12.	P × P	B—Kt 3
13.	Kt—B 3	....

Does Anderssen intend to make a developing move here? Certainly not. That it happens to be one is merely chance. It is essentially an attacking move which threatens 14 Kt × Kt, 15

Q—Q 3, whilst 14 Q—Q 3 can at once be parried by Black with Kt—B 3.

13. ....   Kt (Q 4)—Kt 5
14. B—Kt 1   ....

Diagram V.

14. ....   B—K 3

Morphy could have taken the P at Q 4 but he rightly prefers a simple developing move, otherwise he would have fallen into one of the many complicated traps which Anderssen sets for him.

Let us consider some of the variations—

(a) 14 ...... B×Q P; 15 Kt—K 2, B—Kt 3; 16 P—
R 3 and Q—B 2.

(b) 14 ...... Kt×P!; 15 Kt×Kt, Q×Kt; 16 Q—B 3,
B—K 3; 17 P—R 3, Kt Q 4; 18 R—Q 1.

(c) 14 ...... Kt×P; 15 Kt×Kt, B×Kt!; 16 Q—B 3,
B—K 3; 17 B—K 4, R—Kt 1; 18 P—R 3, &c.

15. P—R 3   Kt—Q 4
16. B—K 3   ....

This also happens to be a developing move only, because with the protection of his pawn at Q 4 the threat involves the gain of a pawn by means of 17 Kt×P, P×Kt; 18 Q—B 2.

16.	....	Kt—B 3
17.	Q—Q 2	R—K 1
18.	R—Q 1	....

To place the Rook not on the open file but on the file blocked by his own pawn seems, according to our present notions, to be very remarkable. But White now threatens P—Q 5 and thereby forces Black to place a piece on Q 4 and as a consequence to move the Kt from B 3 which protects K R 2.

18.	....	B—Q 4

Diagram VI.

19.	Kt—K 5	....

Another of the deep Anderssenian traps. It would have been disastrous for Black to have taken the pawn offered, for 19 Kt×Kt; 20 P×Kt, R×P; 21 B×B, P×B; 22 B—R 2, Q—K 1; 23 Kt×B, Kt×Kt; 24 P—B 4 and White wins. But all this skill is of no assistance, because Morphy by going on with his development undermines more and more White's already weakened centre position.

19.	....	Q—Q 3
20.	Q—B 2	Kt×P
21.	B×Kt	B×B
22.	Kt×B	Q×Kt (K 4)

With this Morphy avoids the last trap. If 22... Q×Kt (Q 4) then 23 Kt—B 6, R—K 5; 24 R×B, R×R; 25 Kt—K 7 ch.

Diagram VII.

| 23. | Kt × Kt ch | Q × Kt |
| 24. | Q—R 7 ch | .... |

Anderssen has thus ultimately carried out his attack along the diagonal Q Kt 1, K R 7. But there is no mate, only a check and Morphy has now a won game.   ....

24.	....	K—B 1
25.	B—K 4	Q R—Q 1
26.	K—R 1	B × Kt P
27.	Q R—Kt 1	R × R ch
28.	R × R	Q × P
29.	Q—R 8 ch	K—K 2
30.	Q—R 7	B—K 4
31.	B—B 3	Q—Kt 6
32.	K—Kt 1	Q—Kt 3

and Black wins by the preponderance of his pawns.

5. THE OPENING

Another of Morphy's perceptions, which becomes clear in a large number of his games, is that superior development increases in value, in proportion as the game is more open.

Therefore the side with the better development should endeavour as much as possible to shape the game as an open one, whilst it is in the interest of the side with the worse development to keep the game close. I give here some characteristic and illustrative games.

White : Morphy.   Black : Amateur.
(Without Q.R.)

	White	Black
1.	P—K 4	P—K 4
2.	Kt—K B 3	Kt—Q B 3
3.	B—B 4	B—B 4
4.	P—Q Kt 4	B × P
5.	P—B 3	B—B 4
6.	P—Q 4	P × P
7.	Castles	B—Kt 3
8.	P × P	P—Q 3

A familiar position in this opening. We see how Morphy is concerned with the possibility of developing moves. Black who plays according to old principles, makes attacking moves—

| 9. | Kt—B 3 | Kt—R 4 |
| 10. | B—Q 3 | B—Kt 5 |

A better development was clearly Kt—K 2, but the text move attacks

| 11. | B—K 3 | Q—B 3 |

An attacking move ; although it is an error in development to bring out the Queen so early in the game.

12.	Kt—Q 5	Q—Q 1
13.	P—K R 3	B × Kt
14.	Q × B	Kt—K B 3

The development comes now too late. Morphy wins with a delightful combination.

15.	B—Kt 5	B × P
16.	P—K 5	B × P
17.	R—K 1	Castles
18.	R × B	P × R
19.	Kt × Kt ch	P × Kt
20.	B × P wins the Queen and the game.	

This game gives us an opportunity also of considering the pawn sacrifice as characteristic of Morphy. Thanks to his principle of development, he often had his Rooks and Bishops in play before his opponent had castled. Those pieces require open lines. The early pawn sacrifices by Morphy are directed towards that object, namely, the opening of lines, and are made mostly for

positional purposes, without any exact calculation. The following game will serve as an
example.

White : Schulten.   Black : Morphy.

1.	P—K 4	P—K 4
2.	P—K B 4	P—Q 4
3.	P × Q P	P—K 5
4.	Kt—Q B 3	Kt—K B 3
5.	P—Q 3	B—Q Kt 5
6.	B—Q 2	P—K 6

Opening the King's file—

7.	B × P	Castles
8.	B—Q 2	B × Kt
9.	P × B	R—K 1 ch
10.	B—K 2	B—Kt 5
11.	P—B 4	P—B 3 !

Foreshadowing the opening of the Queen's file.

12.	P × P	Kt × P
13.	K—B 1	………

Up to this point Morphy had played on positional
lines according to his general principles. But
now comes combination play with accurately
thought out moves of a compelling force.

13.	....	R × B
14.	Kt × R	Kt—Q 5
15.	Q—Kt 1	B × Kt ch
16.	K—B 2	Kt—Kt 5 ch
17.	K—Kt 1	....

Black forces mate in seven moves.

17.	....	Kt—B 6 ch
18.	P × Kt	Q—Q 5 ch
19.	K—Kt 2	Q—B 7 ch
20.	K—R 3	Q × B P ch
21.	K—R 4	Kt—R 3
22.	P—R 3	Kt—B 4 ch
23.	K—Kt 5	Q—R 4 mate.

A large number of still more characteristic and, as regards the development of chess technique, more remarkable games of Morphy had this meaning : that his opponents were unacquainted with the principle that the opening of the game was favourable to the side with the better development, and further that those opponents whose development was defective, in advancing pawns with the object of freeing their position only opened up avenues of mobility for the pieces of the other player.

White : Morphy.   Black : Amateur.

| 1. | P—K 4 | P—K 4 |
| 2. | Kt—K B 3 | K—Q B 3 |

3.	B—B 4	B—B 4
4.	P—Q Kt 4	B × P
5.	P—B 3	B—B 4
6.	P—Q 4	P × P
7.	P × P	B—Kt 3
8.	Castles	Kt—R 4
9.	B—Q 3	P—Q 4

A mistaken advance of the Pawn which opens the King's file for White's Rook and the diagonal R 3—B 8 for White's Q B ; a better move was P—Q 3.

10.	P × P	Q × P
11.	B—R 3	B—K 3
12.	Kt—B 3	Q—Q 2
13.	P—Q 5 !	....

This characteristic pawn sacrifice opens the Queen's file.

13.	....	B × P
14.	Kt × B	Q × Kt
15.	B—Kt 5 ch	Q × B
16.	R—K 1 ch and wins.	

White : Morphy.   Black : Amateur.

1.	P—K 4	P—K 4
2.	Kt—K B 3	Kt—Q B 3
3.	B—B 4	B—B 4
4.	P—Q Kt 4	B × P

5.	P—B 3	B—R 4
6.	P—Q 4	P × P
7.	Castles	P × P
8.	B—R 3	………

The move recommended by theory is Q—Kt 3 ; but the text move corresponds with Morphy's mode of play. The intention is, after Black's P—Q 3, to effect a break through by P—K 5, and to drive home his start in development by a complete opening up of the game.

8.	………	P—Q 3
9.	Q—Kt 3	Kt—R 3
10.	Kt × P	B × Kt
11.	Q × B	Castles
12.	Q R—Q 1	Kt—K Kt 5

already P—K 5 was threatened.

13.	P—R 3	K Kt—K 4
14.	Kt × Kt	Kt × Kt
15.	B—K 2	………

and now P—B 4 to be followed by P—K 5. Of little use would 15 B—Kt 3 have been by reason of the reply B—K 3.

15.	………	P—K B 4

The opening of the game with a defective development is the principal error by which Black loses. P—K B 3 was right. One observes that by reason of the move that was made, namely P—

K B 4, both the King's file as well as the diagonals
Q R 1—K R 8 and Q R 2—K Kt 8 were opened and
to White's advantage, as the latter, thanks to his
better development, is able to occupy them first.

16.	P—B 4	Kt—B 3
17.	B—B 4 ch	K—R 1
18.	B—Kt 2	Q—K 2
19.	Q R—K 1	R—B 3
20.	P×P	Q—B 1

White turns the positional advantage, which he
has been at pains to acquire, into a win, by means
of a wonderfully beautiful combination.

21.	R—K 8	Q×R
22.	Q×R	Q—K 2
23.	Q × P ch	Q×Q
24.	P—B 6 and White wins.	

If 24 .... Q—B 1, then 25 P—B 7 dis. ch, Kt—K 4 ; 26 P ×
Kt, P—R 4 ; 27 P—K 6 dis. ch, K—R 2 ; 28 B—Q 3 ch, K—R
3 ; 29 R—B 6 ch, K—Kt 4 ; 30 R—Kt 6 ch, K—B 5 ; 31 K—B
2 and mate next move.

CHAPTER II

STEINITZ

6. WILHELM STEINITZ

WE have already mentioned that in the old era positional play was almost throughout based on general principles. The perception and development of those general principles were at that time nearly identical with the development of chess playing. From the striving for, and after investigation of, such general principles it becomes clear that chess at that time was treated on scientific lines. The greatest representative of the scientific tendency in chess was Wilhelm Steinitz.

I propose to consider here the difference in the scheme of Morphy's and Steinitz's games respectively. Morphy tried his utmost at the commencement to press forward in the centre, so that his game became open quite early. It was due to his principles of development that he had, in most cases, at the outset a better development than his opponent. As soon, however, as these principles of Morphy's had become the common property of all chess players it was difficult to wrest an advantage in an open game.

On the contrary the old form of opening brought about the early mutual opposing of bishops and rooks and led to simple exchanges. For example, Morphy chose in reply to the French defence the so-called " exchange " variation 1 P—K 4, P—K 3 ; 2 P—Q 4, P—Q 4 ; 3 P×P, P×P, which gives a more open game because the two centre pawns have been got rid of. In this opening Morphy by quick development and mostly for the purpose of doubling his rooks on the only open file, namely, the King's file, used thereby to obtain the command of it ; and that was possible, because his opponent, as a consequence of his failure to develop, was unable to set up an opposition with his rooks in time. This variation of the French defence is looked upon to-day as a typical drawing variation for the reason that by ordinary good play Black is able to put his major pieces in opposition to those of White, and White is then driven to general exchange, should he not wish to relinquish the command of those files, and, thereby, a decisive positional advantage to his opponent. In order to avoid such a simplifying process so early in the game, and to have an opportunity of preparing deeply laid manœuvres for attack, without being threatened by his opponent with exchanges, Steinitz readily chose openings in which he obtained in the centre a more defensive, but strong and unassailable position. The assured centre position afforded him the possibility to prepare a wing attack slowly yet steadily.

In the following match game, Steinitz—Tschigorin, we find this typical scheme of Steinitz play.

7.   STEINITZ—TSCHIGORIN

White : Steinitz.   Black : Tschigorin.

1.	P—K 4	P—K 4
2.	Kt—K B 3	Kt—Q B 3
3.	B—Kt 5	Kt—B 3
4.	P—Q 3	....

One sees here at once the difference between Morphy and Steinitz. The former was always anxious to press on at the earliest possible moment with P—Q 4. Steinitz on the other hand does not want to break through the centre, but is more concerned with building up for himself a strong position, to enable him subsequently to prepare an attack on the King's side.

4.	....	P—Q 3
5.	P—B 3	....

The position of the pawns on Q B 3 and K 4, which makes the forcing of the centre by the Black pieces impossible, runs with regularity through the Steinitz games wherever they are opened with P—K 4.

5. ....   P—K Kt 3
6. Q Kt—Q 2   ....

with the intention of moving the Kt (by way of
Q 2 and B 1) to K 3 or Kt 3 to carry out the attack.
This manœuvre, so much in favour to-day, origin-
ates from Steinitz.   As a fact we find very often
in Steinitz's games these extended Knight manœuvres.   With Morphy, who always brought about
an open game, that kind of manœuvre was impossible ; as he dared not permit himself in open
positions to lose so much time.   Noteworthy and
typical of Steinitz is the delay in castling : so
that the possibility of castling on the Queen's side
remained open to him.

6. ....   B—Kt 2
7. Kt—B 1   Castles
8. B—Q R 4   ....

in order to have this Bishop ready for the attack.
These are all far-reaching and preparatory manœuvres for which in open positions after P—Q 4
there would be no time.

8. ....   Kt—Q 2

with the idea of making the game an open one if
possible by means of Kt—B 4 and P—Q 4.

9. Kt—K 3   Kt—B 4
10. B—B 2   Kt—K 3
11. P—K R 4   ....

Now at this early stage the attack on the King's wing commences and indeed, clearly contrary to Morphy's principles, from an undeveloped position. But the essential point is that Black's counter-play against White's centre does not lend itself to a successful result on account of the latter's assured position. Equally remarkable is it that the move P—K R 4 is not to be found in analagous games of Morphy ; the reason being that Morphy unlike Steinitz always castled early in the game.

> 11. ....   Kt—K 2

after which Black can effectively play P—Q 4.

> 12. P—R 5   P—Q 4
> 13. R P × P   B P × P

Perhaps R P × P was better.   Steinitz would have continued with Q—K 2 in order to avoid exchange of Queens, as one will find happens in similar positions with other players ; at the same time the strong pawn structure formed by the pawns at K 4 and Q B 3 would have been maintained and Black would have gained little by the opening of the Queen's file, as no points of attack are to be found thereon.

After the weakening of the diagonal Q R 2—Kt 8 through B P × P, Steinitz opens that diagonal completely by the exchange on Q 5.

14.	P × P	Kt × P
15.	Kt × Kt	Q × Kt
16.	B—Kt 3	Q—B 3
17.	Q—K 2	B—Q 2
18.	B—K 3	K—R 1
19.	Castles (Q)	Q R—K 1
20.	Q—B 1	....

Apparently a defensive move to provide against Kt—Q 5. In reality preparation for the decision of the contest.

20.	....	P—Q R 4
21.	P—Q 4	....

This ultimately brings the other Bishop on the right diagonal Q R 1—R 8 for the decisive mating attack.

21.	....	P × P
22.	Kt × P	B × Kt

After Kt × Kt, 23 R × Kt equally follows.

23.	R × B	Kt × R
24.	R × P ch	....

After the deep and quiet preparation the end is brought about magnificently, inasmuch as the whole of the pent-up energy becomes active.

24.	....	K × R
25.	Q—R 1 ch	K—Kt 2
26.	B—R 6 ch	K—B 3
27.	Q—R 4 ch	K—K 4
28.	Q × Kt ch and mate next move.	

8. CLOSE POSITIONS

We have seen that Steinitz in his scheme of
play endeavoured, contrary to Morphy, to bring
about a close game. We have also learnt that
the Morphy principle, based on the quick development of pieces, is the correct one only in open
positions. After that had been grasped the next
problem with which players were confronted in
the period of scientific chess was to discover principles upon which close positions could be dealt
with. To have discovered such principles, deeper
and more numerous as they were than those
relating to development in open positions, is
due to Steinitz. The latter, again unlike Morphy,
set forth his thoroughly revolutionary discoveries
concerning chess technique in books on theory,
and also in his analyses of games. He became thereby the founder of a school of chess
which, till a few years ago, was, generally
speaking, the leading one. Steinitz discerned that
in close positions the development of pieces was
not of first importance but that certain continuing
positional characteristics were so. These are
shown by the available material in pieces on the
board and by the structural appearance. His
discoveries are far too comprehensive to permit
of their being fully set out here. But in order to
afford some conception of his ideas I give two of

the games which show frequently-occurring instances of the employment of those positional characteristics already referred to.

9. STEINITZ—MACDONNELL

White : Steinitz.   Black : MacDonnell.

1.	P—K 4	P—K 4
2.	Kt—K B 3	P—Q 3
3.	B—B 4	....

P—Q 4 is usual here. We have already seen, however, that Steinitz did not like to open the game in the centre, but contented himself with a firm unassailable centre position : so that he was free, undisturbed by his opponent to prepare slowly but persistently an attack on the King's wing.

3.	....	B—K 2
4.	P—B 3	Kt—K B 3
5.	P—Q 3	Castles
6.	Castles	B—Kt 5
7.	P—K R 3	B × Kt
8.	Q × B	P—B 3
9.	B—Kt 3	Kt—Q 2
10.	Q—K 2	Kt—B 4
11.	B—B 2	Kt—K 3
12.	P—K Kt 3	Q—B 2

13.	P—K B 4	K R—K 1
14.	Kt—Q 2	Q R—Q 1
15.	Kt—B 3	K—R 1
16.	P—B 5	Kt—B 1

Now Black has a cramped position, because he has too little space in which to arrange his pieces in accordance with *any* plan ; so he moves here and there with an absence of scheme.

17.	P—K Kt 4	P—K R 3
18.	P—Kt 5	P × P
19.	Kt × Kt P	K—Kt 1
20.	K—R 1	Kt (B 3)—R 2
21.	Kt—B 3	....

A most important principle to remember is :— when you control the larger amount of territory do not free the opponent's position by exchanging.

21.	....	R—Q 2
22.	R—K Kt 1	B—Q 1
23.	B—R 6	P—B 3
24.	R—Kt 2	....

The advantage of the greater freedom of space is clearly seen here. White has the possibility, or to put it better, the space for doubling his rooks on to the Kt's file ; Black cannot do likewise.

| 24. | .... | P—Q 4 |

A mistake which hastens Black's defeat. It is however a difficult matter for a player in a cramped position of this kind, in which nothing reasonable can be embarked upon, to avoid making mistakes.

25.	Q R—K Kt 1	R (K 1)—K 2
26.	P × P	P × P
27.	B—R 4	R—Q 3
28.	R × P ch	R × R
29.	R × R ch	Q × R
30.	B × Q	K × B

31. Q—Kt 2 ch and White wins by pre-
    ponderance of material.

10. STEINITZ—BLACKBURNE

White : Steinitz.   Black : Blackburne.

1.	P—K 4	P—K 4
2.	Kt—K B 3	Kt—Q B 3
3.	B—Kt 5	P—Q R 3
4.	B—R 4	Kt—B 3
5.	P—Q 3	P—Q 3
6.	P—B 3	....

Here again the typical Steinitz scheme of play.

6.	....	B—K 2
7.	P—K R 3	....

With this an attack on the King's side is already initiated.

7.	....	Castles
8.	Q—K 2	Kt—K 1
9.	P—K Kt 4	P—Q Kt 4
10.	B—B 2	B—Kt 2
11.	Q Kt—Q 2	Q—Q 2
12.	Kt—B 1	Kt—Q 1
13.	Kt—K 3	Kt—K 3
14.	Kt—B 5	P—Kt 3
15.	Kt × B ch	Q × Kt

When Black played P—K Kt 3 there should have been a Bishop on K Kt 2 to protect the squares B 3 and R 3. Seeing that that Bishop has been exchanged, the squares B 3 and R 3, on which White has now the possibility of establishing pieces, become the so-called weak points in Black's position.

How Steinitz in a few moves avails himself of those weaknesses for his final victory is remarkable.

16.	B—K 3	Kt (K 1)—Kt 2
17.	Castles (Q R)	P—Q B 4
18.	P—Q 4	K P × P
19.	P × P	P—B 5
20.	P—Q 5	Kt—B 2
21.	Q—Q 2	P—Q R 4
22.	B—Q 4	P—B 3
23.	Q—R 6	P—Kt 5

| 24. | P—Kt 5 | P—B 4 |
| 25. | B—B 6 | .... |

Ten moves have taken place since the exchange of Black's K B, and White is firmly established upon the so-called weak points.

25.	....	Q B 2
26.	P×P	P×P
27.	P—Kt 6	Q×Kt P
28.	B×Kt	Q×Q ch

Black must give up the piece, for after 28...Q×B ; 29 R—Kt 1 follows.

29.	B×Q	R—B 3
30.	K R—Kt 1 ch	R—Kt 3
31.	B×P and wins.	

CHAPTER III

THE STEINITZ SCHOOL

II. SIEGBERT TARRASCH

THE ideas of Steinitz were too new for his time. The neglect of development, the extended Knight manœuvres which were bound up with the withdrawal of apparently well posted pieces, the contempt for the momentary as opposed to the permanent positions (more difficult of comprehension), were so remote from his contemporaries that what was original in Steinitz was attributed more to his obstinacy and his preference for what was quaint, rather than to any deep deliberation on his part. But the facts themselves spoke for Steinitz, for he had beaten the best of his contemporaries, namely, Anderssen, Blackburne, Zuckertort and Tschigorin.

The aspiring young Masters of that day began to fashion themselves upon Steinitz's games in preference to those of any others ; and thus arose the Steinitz school. It could not be said to be an imitation of the Steinitz method but rather a combining of the Steinitz technique (not Steinitz's scheme of the game) with the otherwise usual method of playing, whose tendency was the quick development of pieces. The latter Steinitz had neglected. The founder of this new style, the man to give the lead in it, and indeed the most prominent representative of that epoch, is Doctor Siegbert Tarrasch. Furthermore Tarrasch developed another branch of Steinitz's investigations, namely, the correct treatment of the opponent's cramped positions, which was not merely a small or less important branch. The greater freedom of space is by much the most important of the Steinitz permanent positional characteristics. Most of the others (like the advantage of two Bishops or the disadvantage of a weak point on the other side, etc.) may force a cramped position.

It will be remembered that a large number of tournament games of such masters as Maroczy, Schlechter and Teichmann, etc., resembled trench warfare and one perceives also the overwhelming influence of Tarrasch upon the actual development going on in his time. This great influence was due not only to Tarrasch's activity in chess playing but also to his literary achievements.

Contrary to many other masters who kept their methods to themselves, Tarrasch always communicated his theories and his mode of thought in chess to others, and brought them under discussion. In the last decade the general standard of play had risen considerably. A large part of the credit for that can be attributed to

Tarrasch's activity in chess literature. Possibly he could have attained better success as a chess player had he not always published his knowledge and given it to all the others. Still posterity, which will appraise chess not merely as a game but as an art, will judge Tarrasch, not from his material successes (great as they were), but from the intrinsic merit of his performances and from his whole personality.

12.   TARRASCH—SCHLECHTER

White : Dr. Tarrasch.   Black : Schlechter.

1.	P—K 4	P—K 4
2.	Kt—K B 3	Kt —Q B 3
3.	B—Kt 5	P—Q 3

The so-called Steinitz defence against which Tarrasch operates with an energetic system of attack—

4.	P—Q 4	....

White's plan consists of forcing P × P by Black, designated by Tarrasch the " surrender of the centre." Tarrasch, that is to say, had first proved with great force, that the centre pawn formation (White P at K 4, Black's at Q 3) afforded to White the larger amount of freedom of space (see note to Move 8).

4. ....   B—Q 2

Black is at pains to avoid the unfavourable exchange on Q 4 and defends the attacked pawn at K 4 by a counter attack on K 5.

5. Kt—B 3   Kt—B 3

White has covered his Pawn at K 4 and Black has once more attacked it.

6. Castles   B—K 2
7. R—K 1   ....

With this protection of the P at K 4 White forces the surrender of Black's centre.

In a well-known game (Dr. Tarrasch—Marco, Dresden, 1892) mentioned in many books on the opening there occurred 7 ...... Castles; then 8 B × Kt, B × B; 9 P × P, P × P; 10 Q × Q, Q R × Q; 11 Kt × P, B × P; 12 Kt × B, Kt × Kt; 13 Kt—Q 3, P—K B 4; 14 P—K B 3, B—Q 4 ch; 15 Kt × B, Kt × Kt; 16 B—Kt 5 followed by B—K 7 winning.

Diagram VIII.

7. ....   Kt × Q P

In order that Black may exchange not only the
P but also the Kt he loses time because the Q
captures and develops at the same time. Still
this exchange is not to be entirely objected to ;
for generally speaking it is a good plan, in cramped
positions, to free oneself as much as possible, and
one can with limited terrain develop better with
fewer pieces.

The essential error, that causes Schlechter later
on to lose, was his lack of consistency. Whilst,
in the first instance, he seeks in his cramped
position to make matters easier by exchanging,
he afterwards adopts the plan of freeing himself,
generally by advancing his pawns to Q 4 or B 4.
But Black, after the time lost by Kt × P, has no
longer any prospect of carrying through a liberating pawn advance of that nature.

8. Kt × Kt   P × Kt

In order to satisfy ourselves that White, thanks
to the pawn formation (White Pawn at K 4 and
Black P at Q 3) has the freer game I shall now
contrast the respective developing possibilities
of White and Black's pieces.

1 *Rooks*. The White Rooks can be developed
on the Queen and King files : whilst for the Black
Rooks only the Bishop's files are available.

2 *Bishops*.   Whilst the White Bishops are freely mobile, Black's pawn at Q 3 is a block to the Bishop at K 2.

3 *Knights*. The Knights are short-stepping pieces : therefore in order that they may be effective they cannot remain behind like Rooks and Bishops but must seek advanced posts, and they can only assert themselves there if they be protected.   Therefore the destination of the Knights, which is most worth trying to obtain, is the most advanced squares within the protection of their own pawns.   In the position now arrived at in this game, the most advanced squares would be for White Q 5 and K B 5 and for Black Q B 4 and K 4.   We see thus that White has the prospect of posting his Knights permanently on the fifth and Black, on the contrary, only on the fourth. Therefore White's Knight can take part more energetically than can Black's in an attack directed against a castled King.

These positional disadvantages could only be overcome by Black if he succeeded in getting rid of the pawn at K 5 by means of P—Q 4 or P—K B 4.

9.   B × B ch   Q × B

Black could have freed his position much better by Kt × B. The Bishop would thereby have K B 3 free and leave the King's file available for the Rook (at B 1) and the Knight could have been further developed at K 4 or B 4.   After Q × B

Black's cramped position becomes therefore accentuated to the extent that his own pieces stand in the way of one another.   The Queen deprives the Knight at B 3 of the square Q 2 : the Knight blocks the exit for the Bishop at K 2 and the latter closes up for the Rooks the only open file, namely, the King's.

Schlechter, however, took the Bishop with the Queen because with the Q at Q 2 he follows up the impossible plan of carrying out P—Q 4.   To have shown that such a plan is incapable of execution is due to Tarrasch.

10.	Q × P	Castles K R
11.	P—Q Kt 3 !	....

The best way of developing the Bishop 11 B—K Kt 5 would only lead to an exchange and every exchange is to the advantage of the side with the cramped position.

11.	....	K R—K 1
12.	B—Kt 2	B—B 1
(13.	Kt—Q 5 is threatened)	
13.	Q R—Q 1	Q—B 3
14.	R—Q 3	R—K 3
15.	R (Q 3)—K 3	Q R—K 1
16.	P—K R 3	....

This is to prevent Kt—Kt 5.   We observe how the moves that pursue the object of keeping

Black's game cramped, at the same time prepare the decisive attack on the castled King.

16.   ....   Q—Kt 3

17.   Q—Q 3 (of course White will not
                                                    exchange)

17.   ....   P—B 3

The liberating move P—Q 4 is here threatened.

18.   Kt—R 4 !   Q—B 2
19.   P—Q B 4 !   Kt—Q 2
20.   K—R 1   ....

After Kt—Q 2, White has to take into consideration the subsequent possibility of P—K B 4 (which must be checked at the proper time by P—K Kt 4), Tarrasch therefore prefers first to remove the King from the Knight's file (*cf.* note to White's sixteenth move).

20.   ....   P—B 3
21.   Q—B 2   Kt—K 4
22.   Kt—B 3 !   ....

White's intention is to take the badly posted Knight (via K 2 and Q 4) to the favourable square B 5 (*cf.* note to move 8)

22.   ....   Kt—B 2

This move and the following moves of Black are all made with the object of hindering the Knight manœuvre planned by White. In the event of

23 Kt—K 2 Black has an opportunity of making the freeing move P—B 4.

23.   P—K Kt 4   ………

Diagram IX.

23.   ………   Q—R 4

Black, striving to prevent the move Kt—K 2, pays no attention to obtaining his own freedom by P—Q 4. Thus 23—P—Q 4 ; 24 K P × P, R × R ; 25 R × R, R × R ; 26 Kt × R, Q—Kt 3.

24.	R—Q 1	Q—Kt 3
25.	P—K R 4	Kt—K 4
26.	R—Kt 3	Kt—B 2
27.	P—B 3	………

Now Black can no longer prevent Kt—K 2, Q 4—B 5 and assembles in force all his fighting resources on his King's side as a final attempt to parry White's attack.

27.	....	Kt—R 1
28.	Kt—K 2	Q—B 2
29.	Q R—K Kt 1	....

Not 29 Kt—Q 4 at once on account of P—Q 4.

29.	....	Q—B 2
30.	Kt—Q 4	R—K 2
31.	P—K Kt 5	P × P
32.	R × P	P—K Kt 3
33.	Kt—B 5	R—K 4

In desperation, because after any other Rook move 32 Q—B 3 finishes the struggle still more quickly.

34.	P—K B 4

Still in order to continue with Q—B 3 after R × P.

34.	....	R × Kt
35.	P × R	B—Kt 2
36.	P × P	resigns.

13.   TARRASCH—WALBRODT

White : Dr. Tarrasch.   Black : Walbrodt.

1.	P—Q 4	P—Q 4
2.	P—Q B 4	P—K 3
3.	Kt—Q B 3	Kt—K B 3
4.	Kt—B 3	B—K 2
5.	B—B 4	P—B 3

Black contents himself with a cramped but firm position so as to avoid complications and with the hope of thus obtaining a draw. In truth to no other than to Dr. Tarrasch was he so little disposed to concede open terrain. The latter was in taking advantage of such an opportunity inimitably as great as Morphy, having the possibility of a mating attack, or as Steinitz when he espied weak points in the opponent's position.

6.	P—K 3	Q Kt—Q 2
7.	P—K R 3 !	....

In order to avoid the exchange of his Q B for a Knight.

7.	....	Kt—B 1
8.	P—B 5 !	Kt—Kt 3
9.	B—R 2	Q—R 4

A useless sally.

10.	P—R 3	Kt—K 5
11.	B—Q 3	Kt × Kt
12.	Q—Q 2	Kt—K R 5

Following the principle that the player with cramped positions should seek the possibility of exchanging.

13.	Kt × Kt	B × Kt
14.	P—Q Kt 4	Q—Q 1
15.	Q × Kt	Castles
16.	Castles (K R)	Q—Q 2

With the intention of bringing about another exchange by means of B—Q 1 and B 2.

| 17. | Q—B 2 | .... |

The final decision in similar positions must always be carried out by a break-through of pawns, and with that object Tarrasch wants to force the advance of pawns in the castled position in order to have a point of attack ready at hand for such subsequent break-through.

| 17. | .... | P—B 4 |

It is clear now that the break-through on the King's Kt file by means of P—Kt 4 will be feasible.

| 18. | K—R 1 | B—Q 1 |
| 19. | B—K 5 | .... |

White will only submit to the exchange of his
Q B if it means a consequent improvement of his
position.

19.	....	B—B 2
20.	P—B 4	B × B
21.	B P × B	Q—K 2
22.	P—Kt 4 !	P—Kt 3
23.	R—B 4	....

It is important to mention here that if White
played at once P × P, Black would reply with
Kt P × P. Should White then bring his major
pieces to bear on the Kt file, Black opposes him
on that file and White achieves nothing.

The more open position on the Kt file White
rightly takes advantage of first, by placing his
major pieces on it, where Black, by reason of
his obviously increasing lack of terrain, cannot
oppose him, and then by exchanges.

23.	....	B—Q 2
24.	R—K Kt 1	K—R 1
25.	Q—Kt 2	P—Q R 4

This attempt at an assault upon White's Queen's
wing proves unsuccessful because Black must
keep his Rook in readiness for use at any moment
for the defence of his threatened King's wing.

26.	B—Kt 1	R P × P
27.	R P × P	R—R 5
28.	P × P	....

Just at the right moment. For after 28...Kt P×P; 29 R—B 3 followed by R—Kt 3 and R—Kt 7 would soon decide the issue. Black is therefore forced, as a sequence to R—R 5, to take with the King's pawn, and his close position on the Kt's file becomes thereby stabilised. Thereupon White's K P becomes a protected passed pawn.

28.	....	K P×P
29.	Q—Q 2	R—K Kt 1
30.	Q—K 1 !	....

The continuation of the storming operation by pawns against the constricted King's position of the other side is here prepared.

30.	....	B—K 3
31.	P—R 4	Q R—R 1
32.	R (B 4)—B 1	....

White by this move and the next few moves does not dispose of his pieces so as to arrive at a decision of the fight in the quickest possible way. In such positions, however, breathing time is permissible, seeing that the opponent is crippled.

32.	....	R—Kt 2
33.	R—Kt 2	Q R—K Kt 1
34.	R—K R 2	Q—Q 2

35.	B—Q 3	R—R 1
36.	Q—Kt 3	Q—K 2
37.	R—K Kt 1	Q R—K Kt 1
38.	R(R 2)—K Kt 2	R—K B 1
39.	Q—B 4	R (B 1)—K Kt 1
40.	Q—R 6	B—Q 2
41.	K—R 2 ! !	....

The direct break-through by means of B—K 2 and P—R 5 would with Black's firm position lead only to a general exchange of pieces and to a drawn end game. Tarrasch now applies his finest and last resources.

He avails himself of the large amount of open spaces at his disposal to bring his King to the middle of the board before those exchanges take place, which Black with his close formation is unable to emulate. It is on that account that the ensuing end game terminates in White's favour with such rapidity.

41.	....	B—K 3
42.	R—Kt 5	B—Q 2
43.	K—Kt 3	B—K 1
44.	K—B 4	B—Q 2
45.	P—R 5	B—K 1
46.	P × P	B × P
47.	B—K 2	Q—Q 1
48.	B—R 5	B × B

Another trap—If R × R then Q—R 5 ch.

49.	Q × B	R × R
50.	R × R	R × R
51.	Q × R	Q—K B 1
52.	P—K 6	Resigns.

14. EMANUEL LASKER

DURING the era of scientific chess there were not only accurate investigators like Steinitz and Tarrasch who built up their theories on experience, but there was living at that time a philosopher who played chess, by name Emanuel Lasker: the former chess champion. In giving a portrayal of Lasker's individuality in chess I must not omit therefrom his love of philosophy. He began with quite small essays and lectures in which he compared chess to life. Then he wrote an essay entitled " der Kampf " (The Struggle). To struggle means to overcome difficulties which stand in the way of reaching a goal. He tried to discover general laws for the proper way to carry on the struggle. Chess as an example of a purely intellectual and straightforward struggle he adduced as the test of the correctness of his theory. Lasker's chess activities were not an end in themselves, but a preparation for his philosophy. It strikes one as remarkable that Lasker, the one-time world's chess champion, had no disciples.

Steinitz had founded a school. Nearly all modern masters have learnt from Tarrasch. One perceives quite clearly the mind of young Rubinstein in the chess praxis of later years: Only Lasker is inimitable. Why is it? We ask: Can he be said to have given us nothing lasting towards the progress of our game?

The other masters endeavoured to create a specific chess technique. They studied the peculiarity of the board and of the pieces and propounded general maxims such as " two Bishops are stronger than two Knights" or " the Rook should be placed behind the passed pawns." Those are maxims that have no general value and, to a great extent, so far as they apply to progressive chess technique, require certain qualification: yet they are glasses for the short-sighted and have their uses. Lasker acknowledged only universal laws of the struggle and by means thereof he triumphed over Steinitz and Tarrasch and proved the errors and defects in their chess technique. Therein lay his merit in chess. So to improve his powers, that attack and the necessary defence went hand in hand, was for Lasker not a matter of chess principle only. The latter troubled him but little. It was the struggle as such that concerned him. But against the most perfect technique even the Titans with their bare strength could not prevail. Thus Lasker was beaten by Capablanca. The age of heroes is over in chess, as well as in other things. Where Lasker was most original was in his application of the principles of development. Take, for example, with what wonderful control he avoids the self suggesting and attractive moves for the sake of correct development.

Diagram **X.**

This position arises out of the Ruy Lopez opening, viz. : in a game Lasker—Janowski and in a game Schlechter—Lasker.

1.	P—K 4	P—K 4
2.	Kt—K B 3	Kt—Q B 3
3.	B—Kt 5	Kt—K B 3
4.	Castles	P—Q 3
5.	P—Q 4	B—Q 2
6.	Kt—B 3	B—K 2
7.	R—K 1	P × P

8.	Kt × P	Castles
9.	B × Kt	P × B
10.	B—Kt 5	R—K 1
11.	P—K R 3	P—K R 3
12.	B—R 4	Kt—R 2
13.	B × B	Q × B
14.	Q—B 3	………

It is clear that the Knight at R 2 is not sufficiently effective. Janowski did what most would
have done, namely, he brought the Knight for
an attack on the Queen by way of Kt 4 to K 3
without any loss of time. But on K 3 the Knight
is not favourably placed, because it blocks both
the King's file and the outlet for the Bishop at
Q 2. Lasker therefore renounces the apparent
gain of time by 14...Kt—Kt 4 for the sake of
correct   development,   and   played   against
Schlechter 14...Kt—B 1 (so as to get the Knight
to Kt 3) and obtained a good game after 15 Q R—
Q 1, Kt—Kt 3 ; 16 Q—Kt 3, Q—Kt 4.

15.   MARSHALL—LASKER

White : Marshall.   Black : Lasker.

	White	Black
1.	P—K 4	P—K 4
2.	Kt—K B 3	Kt—Q B 3
3.	B—Kt 5	Kt—B 3
4.	P—Q 4	P × P
5.	Castles	B—K 2
6.	P—K 5	Kt—K 5
7.	Kt × P	Castles
8.	Kt—B 5	P—Q 4
9.	B × Kt	P × B
10.	Kt × B ch	Q × Kt
11.	R—K 1	Q—R 5
12.	B—K 3	P—B 3

Black develops the Rook (B 1) with this move : at the same time it serves as an introduction to an exceedingly deep combination, with a sacrifice which follows. One discerns very often in Lasker's games how he seized the idea of a combination in striving to continue his development untroubled by the threats of his opponent, his superior development frustrating his opponent's threat.

13.	P—K B 3	P × P
14.	P × Kt	P—Q 5

Diagram XI.

15. P—K Kt 3 ....

The Bishop dare not move, *e.g.*, 15 B—Q 2, B—
Kt 5 ; 16 Q—B 1, R—B 7 ; 17 B—Kt 5, R ×
P ch ! ; 18 K × R, B—R 6 ch ; 19 K—R 1, Q—
B 7, or, 15 B—B 1, Q—B 7 ch ; 16 K—R 1,
B—Kt 5.

Had Marshall only rightly seen that he was
forced after P—Kt 3 to give back the Bishop it
would have been better for him to have done so
at once with 15...Q—K 2.

15. .... Q—B 3
16. B × P ....

The depth of Lasker's combination is appreciated
if we probe here the consequences of 16 B—Q 2.
Then would follow Q—B 7 ch ; 17 K—R 1, B—
R 6 ; 18 R—Kt 1, P—R 4 ! (threatening B—Kt 5

and B 6 ch) 19 Q × P (or B—K 1), Q × R ch ; 20
K × Q, R—B 8 mate.

16.	....	P × B
17.	R—B 1	Q × R ch
18.	Q × Q	R × Q ch
19.	K × R	....

Marshall might have thought that he stood well
in the end game on account of Black's doubled
pawns, but Black's better development decides
the issue in his favour.

| 19. | .... | R—Kt 1 |

This discarding of apparent development with
a gain of time through B—R 6 ch exhibits Lasker's
deep insight into the essence of good development.
The Bishop, as a preliminary, is posted best on
B 1 because from there it operates in two directions.   We shall see from what follows (cf. note
to White's twenty-first move) how both of these
directions come to be of value.

| 20. | P—Kt 3 | R—Kt 4 |

The Rook is developed on the open rank.

| 21. | P—B 4 | .... |

The next best move 21 Kt—Q 2 would not have
been good because R—Q B 4 ; 22 R—B 1, B—
R 3 ch and B—Q 6. Here the one possibility of
developing the Bishop can be turned to account

although as a fact it is subsequently developed
on the other side (see move 27).

21.	....	R—K R 4
22.	K—Kt 1	....

If 22 P—K R 4, P—Kt 4 ; 23 P × P, R—R 8 ch and White
is crippled.

22.	....	P—B 4

Now Black has gained the advantage of a protected passed Pawn.

23.	Kt—Q 2	K—B 2 !

develops the King before he gets cut off by R—B 1

24.	R—B 1 ch	K—K 2
25.	P—Q R 3	R—R 3 !

As the fourth Rank is no longer quite free the
Rook is brought on to the third Rank.

26.	P—K R 4	R—R 3
27.	R—R 1	B—Kt 5
28.	K—B 2	K—K 3
29.	P—R 4	K—K 4
30.	K—Kt 2	R—K B 3
31.	R—K 1	P—Q 6

The passed Pawn protected by the King wins.

32.	R—K B 1	K—Q 5
33.	R × R	P × R
34.	K—B 2	P—B 3

Black makes moves to gain time because the White pieces have only forced moves.

35.	P—Q R 5	P—Q R 3
36.	Kt—B 1	K × P
37.	K—K 1	B—K 7
38.	Kt—Q 2 ch	K—K 6
39.	Kt—Kt 1	P—B 4
40.	Kt—Q 2	P—R 4
41.	Kt—Kt 1	K—B 6

and Black wins.

16. TARRASCH—LASKER

White : Tarrasch.   Black : Lasker.

1.	P—K 4	P—K 4
2.	Kt—K B 3	Kt—Q B 3
3.	B—Kt 5	Kt—B 3
4.	Castles	P—Q 3
5.	P—Q 4	B—Q 2
6.	Kt—B 3	B—K 2
7.	R—K 1	P × P
8.	Kt × P	....

A position is arrived at in which White can develop his striking forces on the first four to five ranks whilst Black has only three at his disposal (compare the treatment of this position in Chapter XXII). Black finds himself on that account cramped and seeks by means of exchanges to free his game.

8.	....	Kt × Kt
9.	Q × Kt	B × B
10.	Kt × B	....

We now get in accordance with well-known principles the following developing moves on each side.

10.	....	Castles
11.	B—Kt 5	R—K 1
12.	Q R —Q 1	P—K R 3
13.	B—R 4	Kt—Q 2

The Knight is badly posted at B 3 because Black cannot challenge the control of K 5 and Q 4. Besides it stands in the way of the Bishop at K 2, whilst the Bishop itself blocks the only open file for the Rook.   For that reason and to bring about a further exchange 13...Kt—Q 2 occurs.

14.	B × B	R × B
15.	Q—B 4	....

White has developed all his pieces even to the Kt at Q Kt 5 which he wants to convey to K B 5 by way of Q 4.

15.	....	R—K 4 ! !

After this move White clearly dare not take the pawn at Q B 7.

Diagram XII.

In this position Black by numerous exchanges has somewhat overcome the disadvantage of his cramped position. That is to say a disadvantage merely as contrasted with White's position. Whilst White has the King and Queen's files at his disposal for the development of both his Rooks, Black has only the King's file open. Black is therefore confronted with the difficulty arising from his inability to turn both Rooks to account. How does Lasker meet those difficulties? He has recourse to an idea which may not strike the layman as being anything extraordinary, but which to the expert seems as original as it is bold. He wants to get his Rook into the open, via K 4, well knowing that not only would any attacks by

White against him be of no avail but that he can
harass effectually White's Queen's side.

16.	Kt—Q 4	R—Q B 4 !
17.	Q—Kt 3	Kt—Kt 3

The Knight is necessary for the support of the
Rook as will be seen from the course of the game.

18.	P—K B 4	....

Tarrasch's execution in this game is not on the
same level as that of his opponent. He does not
carry out any counter action but does the most
obvious thing. He cuts off the Rook, which he
considers badly positioned, from the squares
available in the event of its having to retire, and
above all from K 4. But Lasker had no intention
of bringing back the Rook to the King's file so
soon, he having just moved it to Q B 4.

18.	....	Q—B 3
19.	Q—K B 3	R—K 1
20.	P—B 3	P—Q R 4

In order to attack the Queen's wing with P—
Q R 5, Q R 6.

21.	P—Q Kt 3	....

so as to shut the Rook in completely after P—R 5
with P—Q Kt 4 without Black being able to take
the Pawn *en passant*.

| 21. | .... | P—R 5 |
| 22. | P—Q Kt 4 | R—B 5 |

Now there is no move for the Rook.

| 23. | P—Kt 3 | .... |

Protecting pawn at B 4 and to make the Queen mobile.

| 23. | .... | R—Q 1 |

This move discloses at once the weakness of White's Queen's side and at the same time the strength of the Rook's position at B 5. Black now threatens, with P—Q B 4, to burst open White's Queen wing and to liberate his own Rook and further to reap an advantage from the weakness of White's Pawns. It would have been a mistake to play at once P—Q B 4 because of the counter-attacking move 24 Kt—Kt 5.

| 24. | R—K 3 | .... |

White is now positionally outplayed. He has, as against the threat 24...P—Q B 4 no defence from a positional point of view. Therefore he attempts to create one by means of a combination, which, as is usual with all combinations resorted to in a state of mere desperation, does not get home. We shall very soon see that 24 R—K 3 is the necessary preparation with which to meet the designed combination of 24...P—B 4. (Cf. note to White's 27th move).

24.	....	P—B 4
25.	Kt—Kt 5	P × P
26.	R × P	....

Here comes the combination.

26.	....	R × R
27.	P—K 5	....

If the Rook at K 3 now stood at K 1 Black would obtain the advantage by 27...Q—K 2 ; 28 Kt × R, R × Q B P.

27.	....	R × K B P

A surprising move which upsets White's combination. Whatever White plays Black retains a pawn preponderance.

28.	Kt P × R	Q—Kt 3 ch

and Black won through his pawn preponderance on the Queen's side.

What is it, we may well ask, in this game that pleases us so much. The layman who plays it through without any enlightenment will at most derive some interest from the surprise move 27... R × K B P. But the expert will with very great tension follow Lasker's equally original and deep idea of placing his Rook upon seemingly perilous ground in order to extricate himself from his congested position. And we experience a desire that this bold stroke of genius, and not the sober prosaic method will snatch a victory.

We see how Tarrasch, the man of method, closes in the Rook that has been forced through. We were just on the point of giving up Black's game as lost. It was Black who had our sympathy. But then comes a surprising move 23...R—Q I ; with the threat of liberating the Rook and breaking up White's position, and then again White's counter combination. The drama approaches its climax. And then when the solution comes 27... R×B P ; great is our delight that the miraculous has really come to pass and that the idea of a genius, for which every pedagogue would have foretold a bad end, has triumphed over all that was systematic and according to rule.

We saw at the commencement of this book that the pleasure derived by the chess lover from sacrificial combinations was the feeling that with them mind triumphs over matter. To play for material advantage is what everybody does. It is the usual everyday occurrence and may be deemed banal.

But winning combinations involving sacrifices, on the contrary, represent to us the victory of genius over what is banal or over that jejune practical mind which seeks but to harvest every material advantage. The chess votary thus sees in the sacrifice the miraculous about which he dreams, but which as a rule he never meets with. Now we appreciate that what affords us so much enjoyment in chess is really the same thing for all

of us, be it for the layman who sees nothing finer
in chess than the sacrificial combination or be it
for the expert who marvels at the far-reaching
scheme of a game. It is the triumph of the
intellect and genius over lack of imagination ;
the triumph of personality over materialism.

17.   AMERICANISM IN CHESS

THE difference between European and American
intellectual life had to find itself also in chess.
I shall contrast here two masters, and contemporaries, as representatives of the antithesis,
namely, Rudolf Charousek and Harry Nelson
Pillsbury. I once wrote the following sketch of
Charousek—" Youth has still its dreams and
its ideals : but in the struggle for life they wear
off. The ordinary citizen soon gets immersed in
the troubles of everyday life and in its sorrows
and joys. The right man is he who stands firm
by his own ideas ; they form the main support of
his life and his labours. Still there comes a time
when he may renounce them and run his head
against the wall. He adapts himself to stern
necessity : tardily, gradually, and by a circuitous
path does he bring his goal by ever so little within
his reach.

" But seldom do we meet with the man who is
so child-like, yet so great, as to disregard the sharp

edges of reality even when they hurt him. His dreams for him are actualities, he walks straight out towards his goal to which no road leads. On that account, to those who come after him, does his performance seem so incomprehensively simple.

" It is a delight to watch a young and gifted chess player. To him have come no sinister experiences ; to him continual carping care is foreign. Therefore he loves the attack and the bold sacrifice ; for therein lies the shortest way to his ultimate objective.

" But that state of things does not last long and through failure he becomes wise. Soon the boldness disappears : we find him more concerned with safety and he gathers in the advantages which come into his hands direct. In that way the majority of people play. Here and there we find a player, who is not so easily cowed by untoward experiences. He is still rich in plans, but he bears in mind that he is not playing alone. Therefore he is careful and gets to love the readymade roads, at the most improving them. In that way does the master play.

" It was otherwise with Charousek. He had to carry out his ideas. He knew no opponent : he only knew his goal. When he ran his head against a wall, he found its weak points and went right through. Always going straight ahead, his execution appears to us to be most simple.

And yet no one could emulate him in this very simplicity."

Is the picture I have just drawn really that of Charousek ? No indeed ; it is only an ideal, the idealistic picture of a chess master as it floats before my eyes : an ideal to which the real Charousek perhaps approached.

For such is the strength and weakness of the European thinker and plodder, that he always strives after the impossible. The American is steady and turns what is possible to account. The great American chess masters (Morphy, Mackenzie, Pillsbury) astonished the world by their successes at their first appearances. Morphy retired early from chess : Mackenzie and Pillsbury in the long run were bound to acknowledge the greater depth of the world champions Steinitz and Lasker. To the European mind has undoubtedly belonged the past ; possibly to Americans belong the present and the future.

Pillsbury in his play was a true American. His games, free from all plodding depth of thought and simple in their scheme, show astonishingly big lines in their undertakings and have a refreshing effect upon the onlooker through the energy in their execution. Pillsbury was a disciple of Steinitz : but the latter's persistent seeking and plodding was foreign to Pillsbury's character. He adopted indeed the complete practical results of the Steinitz theories and the latter formed the groundwork of Pillsbury's technique.

Pillsbury is most wonderful when he sets himself out to exploit weaknesses in a hostile position. Then does his play on big lines assert itself ; not content with storing up small advantages, he always finds the right method for destroying his opponent's position root and branch.   His games attained a height above the ordinary level and placed Pillsbury in the rank of the great masters.

18.   BLACKBURNE—CHAROUSEK

White : Blackburne.   Black : Charousek.

1.	P—Q 4	P—Q 4
2.	Kt—K B 3	P—K 3
3.	B—B 4	B—Q 3

If White chooses not to play like Rubinstein P—K 3 he is bound here, either through the exchange or the withdrawal of the Bishop, to lose time.   Black thereby succeeds in first moving the King's pawn.

4.	B × B	Q × B
5.	Q Kt—Q 2	Kt—K B 3

6.	P—B 3	Q Kt—Q 2
7.	Q—B 2	P—K 4
8.	P—K 3	Castles
9.	P × P	....

White exchanges so as not to be forced always to have to think about an eventual P—K 5.

| 9. | .... | Kt × P |
| 10. | B—K 2 | .... |

Now White's difficulties increase : it would have been better for him to have renounced the possibilities of freeing his game by P—B 4 or P—K 4 and to have simplified his game by Kt × Kt, Q × Kt ; 11 Kt—B 3

10.	....	B—Kt 5
11.	P—K R 3	B—R 4
12.	Kt × Kt	....

White is cramped and the threat of B—Kt 3 is before him.

12.	....	B × B
13.	K Kt —B 3	Q—R 3
14.	Kt—Kt 3	B—Q 6
15.	Q—Q 1	P—Q Kt 3
16.	Kt—B 1	B—B 5 ! !

Very fine ! If instead 16...B—Kt 3 then Q—K 2 follows.

17.   Kt—K 5   ....

After 17 P—Q Kt 3 would come Q—R 4 ; 18 Q—Q 2, B—R 3.

17.	....	Q R—Q 1
18.	Q—B 2	Q—Kt 2
19.	Kt—K 2	K R—K 1
20.	Kt × B	P × Kt
21.	Castles (K R)	Q—K 5

After the exchange of Queens, Black's superiority becomes clear.

22.	Q × Q	Kt × Q
23.	K R—Q 1	P—K Kt 4

Charousek wants to restrict the White Knight. With that object however 23...P—Q B 4 would have been better—thus 24 Kt—B 4, Kt—Q 7 and White is absolutely crippled.

24.	Kt—Q 4	R—Q 4
25.	Kt—B 3	R—Q 6

Charousek must have over-looked with 23...P—Kt 4 that he would now attain nothing by K R—Q 1 on account of 26...R—Q 4.

26.	Kt—K 1	R (Q 6)—Q 1
27.	Kt—B 3	P—Q B 4

28.	K—B 1	P—Kt 4
29.	P—R 3	P—Q R 4
30.	K—K 2	P—Q Kt 5
31.	R P × P	R P × P
32.	R × R	R × R
33.	P × P	P—B 6

Better than 33...P × P; 34 Kt—Q 4! But in spite of the remarkably fine play, Black after the mistake of his twenty-third move, can no longer win the beautifully planned game.

34.	P (Kt 2) × P	Kt × P ch
35.	K—K 1	P × P
36.	Kt—Q 4	R—Kt 1
37.	Kt—Kt 3	K—Kt 2
38.	R—R 6	P—R 4

Charousek sets himself out to make White's King's wing the object of an attack.

39.	P—Kt 3	R—Q B 1
40.	Kt—Q 4	R—B 4
41.	R—R 7	K—Kt 3
42.	R—Kt 7	R—R 4
43.	R × Kt P	R—R 8 ch
44.	K—Q 2	Kt—K 5 ch
45.	K—K 2	R—R 7 ch
46.	K—B 3	Kt × B P

Diagram XIII.

White dare not now play 47 R—Kt 6 ch, P—B 3 ; 48 P—R 4 on account of P—Kt 5 ch ; 49 K—B 4, Kt—R 8. It looks as if Charousek has gained another advantage, but here Blackburne also exhibits his skill in the clearest light.

47.	R—Kt 6 ch	P—B 3
48.	P—Kt 4 ! !	P—R 5
49.	R—Kt 7	Kt × R P
50.	Kt—K 6	....

The point. 50 Kt—B 5 would have been wrong on account of Kt—Kt 8 ch ; 51 K—K 4, R—R 5 ch with the text move 51 Kt—B 8 ch and R—R 7 mate are threatened.

50.	....	Kt—Kt 8 ch
51.	K—K 4	R—R 5 ch
52.	K—Q 3	R—R 1

After R × P a mate of the problem type with 53 Kt—B 8 would follow in two moves.

53.	R—Kt 7 ch	K—R 3
54.	R—B 7	R—K Kt 1
55.	R × P ch	R—Kt 3
56.	R—B 1	drawn.

19. PILLSBURY—TARRASCH

We all know the dramas of the American films in which we witness danger approaching. With breathless tension the audience look for some deed or happening that will bring about salvation, but it seems to be too late for that. Only at the last moment, and just in time, the situation is saved. Such an exciting drama is afforded us in the following game. After White's twenty-eighth move the position shown in Diagram 14 was arrived at.

Diagram XIV.

Tarrasch played

28. ⋯⋯⋯   Q—R 5

which appears to be decisive: for after 29 Kt—
B 1, Q—B 7; Black would take possession of
White's Queen's wing. But Pillsbury kept his
opponent thoroughly occupied by

29. Kt—Kt 4!   ⋯⋯⋯

threatening the sacrifice of the Knight at B 6—
Black replies therefore with

29. ⋯⋯⋯   Kt—Q 2

It went on

30. R (B 4)—B 2!   ⋯⋯⋯

Still Black dare not take the Pawn at R 7 because after that Pillsbury would win by 31 Kt—B 4, B—B 2 ; 32 Kt—Kt 6 ch, B × Kt ; 33 P × B, Kt—B 1 (33...P—R 3 ? ; 34 Kt × R P, P × Kt ; 35 Q × R P ch, K—Kt 1 ; 36 R—B 4) 34 Kt × P, P × Kt ; 35 R × P, K—Kt 1 ; 36 R—B 7 wins. To thwart this threat Black played

30. ....   K—Kt 1

and in that way Pillsbury had gained time

31. Kt—B 1   ....

to ward off the worst : for now Black's Q—Q 7 is prevented.   But of what use is it in the long run ?   Black plays

31. ....   P—B 6

so as after

32. P—Q Kt 3   Q—B 3

to continue with P—Q R 4, R 5 and P × P ; P × P, R—R 1, R 6 ; in order to deprive White of material on the Queen's wing, whereafter Black's pawns would win easily.   Ought White to take up a defensive attitude ?   Had he done so, he later on would have found himself at a disadvantage.

33.　P—K R 3　　.........

Pillsbury had reckoned out exactly the time always at his command and prepares his counter-blow with all calmness.

33.　.........　　P—Q R 4
34.　Kt—R 2　　.........

This appears to the audience to be tormentingly slow.

34.　.........　　P—R 5
35.　P—Kt 4　　P × P
36.　P × P　　R—R 1
37.　P—Kt 5　　R—R 6
38.　Kt—Kt 4　　B × P

One would think that White is lost.　But at the last moment comes the catastrophe that is to annihilate Black.

39.　R—K Kt 2　　.........

which threatens not only P × P but also Kt × P dis. ch after.

39.　.........　　K—R 1
40.　P × P　　P × P

if the Knight takes, then 41 Kt—K 5 settles matters.

41.	Kt × B	R × Kt
42.	Kt—R 6	R—Kt 2

The only move

43.	R × R	K × R
44.	Q—Kt 3 ch	K × Kt
45.	K—R 1 ! !	....

The *deus ex machina*. Black can only with the heaviest sacrifices avert the early impending mate by 46 R—K Kt 1.

45.	....	Q—Q 4
46.	R—K Kt 1	Q × B P
47.	Q—R 4 ch	Q—R 4
48.	Q—B 4 ch	Q—Kt 4
49.	R × Q	P × R
50.	Q—Q 6 ch	K—R 4
51.	Q × Kt and wins.	

20.   CARL SCHLECHTER

VIENNA, the old art city, was always the city of those who were unrecognised or of those whose recognition came too late. That is ingrained in the spirit of everything that goes to make up Vienna and Viennese Art.   For that art is wanting in the grand pathos and tragic gesture. It is not blatant; on the contrary it is hidden. It does not impose itself: it has rather to be approached; it must be sought out. Vienna has an old chess tradition, because chess is particularly the game of the unappreciated, who seek in play that success which life has denied them.

Steinitz sprang from the chess school of Vienna, but to become the world champion he went abroad and divested himself of what was Viennese in him. The most noted representative of the Viennese in chess was Schlechter. He showed himself quite equal to Lasker the World Champion, but he was too Viennese to wrest the title of World's Champion. The majority of people imagine a chess master as being a townsman who passes his life in an atmosphere of smoke and play in cafés and clubs: a neurasthenic individual, whose nerves and brains are continually working at tension: a one-sided person who has given up his whole soul to chess.

Schlechter was the exact antithesis of that conception. He held himself aloof from club and café, so far as his vocation permitted. He lived for preference in the country, where he filled in his leisure with art and science. All his heart and soul went out to nature, and it is just that reflex of his love of nature that lends to his games their particular charm. His games stand out through their breadth of scheme—just as in the forest the trunks of trees and their branches stretch themselves out on all sides wherever there are open spaces : thus did Schlechter develop his forces ; forcibly and, like Nature as it were, objectless. No hidden places and traps were there, but only sound development. With him was no undue haste and no pinning himself down to one idea, but one harmonious evolution. And indeed combinations by Schlechter are not artificially-reared roses which amaze everyone with their beauty and which, to the true nature lover, soon savour of excess ; nay, they are rather the humble and hidden forest flowers that have to be looked for and the love of which increases with their gathering. Thus one loses one's self in Schlechter's games in which are reflected, side by side with the immensity and simplicity of nature, the airiness of Viennese art and music.

By the time we shall have grown weary of the blatant combinations of the old masters and the over subtle positional plans of the new ones, we shall still delight in immersing ourselves in Schlechter's games, in which, side by side with the greatness and simplicity of nature, the grace and airiness of Viennese music are often reflected.

21.   SCHLECHTER—JOHN

Schlechter's art is to be compared with that of writers of stories and of the composers of epics.

He does not rush like Mieses, for example, to make original points : nor does he, as Tarrasch sometimes does, try by means of great ornamentation to produce the appearance of profundity. Schlechter treats all parts of the game and of the board with equal care and liking.

The following game is one of the most beautiful, although little known, examples of that broad design, which thanks to his style of play is to be found in his games.

White : Schlechter.   Black : John.

1.	P—Q 4	P—Q 4
2.	P—Q B 4	P—K 3
3.	Kt—Q B 3	P—K B 4
4.	Kt—B 3	P—B 3

The weakness of the stonewall defence lies in the shutting off of the Queen's Bishop. In the game now before us the Black game ultimately fails by reason of that weakness.

5.	B—B 4	B—Q 3
6.	P—K 3 ! !	Kt—B 3
7.	B—Q 3	Q—B 2
8.	P—K Kt 3 !	....

White's handling of the opening, with the idea after 8...B×B; 9 K P×B of exerting pressure on the King's file, originated with Pillsbury.

8.	....	Castles
9.	Castles	Kt—K 5
10.	Q—Kt 3	K—R 1
11.	Q R—B 1	B×B

Black loses patience and opens for White his King's file : for otherwise he sees staring him in the face, 12 P×P, K P×P; 13 Kt—Q Kt 5.

12.	K P×B	Q—B 2
13.	Kt—K 5	Q—K 2
14.	B×Kt !	....

Now Schlechter apparently blocks the King's file. As a fact he opens it again with his following move in a favourable way.

14.	....	B P×B
15.	P—B 3	K P×P
16.	Q R—K 1 !	Q—Q B 2

White threatened P×P and Kt×P.

17.	Q—R 3	K—Kt 1

If Black plays 17...Kt—Q 2 White cripples him with Q—K 7.

18.	R × P	Kt—R 3
19.	P—Kt 3 !	Q—Q 1
20.	P—Q B 5	Kt—B 2
21.	Q—Kt 2	B—Q 2
22.	Q—Q B 2	Q—K 2
23.	R (K 1)—B 1	Q R—K 1
24.	P—K Kt 4	B—B 1
25.	R—R 3 !	....

By which White forces weak points in Black's position.

25.	....	P—K Kt 3
26.	P—Kt 4	....

It is surprising that White suddenly begins an attack on the Queen's side. But that is the epic of Schlechter's game mentioned at the commencement of this chapter. He carries out operations apparently not concerted on different parts of the board, so that one has the impression that a game with no clear preconceived objective is in progress. And it is only at the end that one perceives for the first time the connection of things seemingly disconnected, with the result that the game is rounded off into one great homogeneous whole.

26.	....	Q—B 3
27.	R (R 3)—B 3	R—K 2

28.	P—Q R 4	P—Q R 3
29.	Kt—Q 1 ! !	....

By move 25 White forced the weakening of K B 3 and K R 3 in Black's position. Now the Knight migrates towards one of those points, namely, White's R 6.

29.	....	R—Kt 2
30.	Kt—K 3	Q—K 2
31.	P—K Kt 5	B—Q 2
32.	Kt (K 3)—Kt 4	B—K 1
33.	Kt—R 6 ch	K—R 1
34.	Q—K 2	....

Black has three weak points on the King's side. On two of them (K 4 and R 3) White is firmly established. In order to take advantage of the third (B 3) White wants to place his Queen on his K 5 in lieu of the Knight and to bring that liberated Knight to Black's B 3.

34.	....	Q—Q 1
35.	Kt (K 5)—Kt 4	B—Q 2
36.	Q—K 5	Kt—K 1
37.	R—K R 3	Q—B 2

If 37 ...... Q—K 2 then Q—Kt 8 wins.

| 38. | Kt—B 6 ! | .... |

Diagram XV.

38.	....	Q×Q

If 38 ... Q—Q 1 then 39 Kt×R P!; if 38 ... B—B 1; 39 Kt×Kt, Q×Q; 40 B P×Q, R×Kt; 41 R (R 3) —B 3.

39.	B P×Q	R—K 2
40.	R (R 3)—K B 3	Kt×Kt
41.	R×Kt	R×R
42.	K P×R	R—K 1
43.	Kt—B 7 ch	K—Kt 1
44.	Kt—K 5	R—Q 1
45.	K—Kt 2	K—B 1
46.	P—R 4	B—K 1

Now we see that White by his attack has arrived at a solution, after which Black, in consequence of his original and permanently

disadvantageous position involving the blocking
in of his Bishop by his own chain of pawns,
must lose.

47.	K—B 3	B—B 2
48.	K—B 4	K—K 1
49.	R—Q Kt 1	....

The attack on the Queen's side for some time
interrupted is now resumed and brings about a
speedy termination.

49.	....	K—B 1
50.	P—Kt 5	Resigns.

If

50.	......	R P × P
51.	P × P	B—K 1
52.	P × P	B × P
53.	Kt × B	P × Kt
54.	K—K 5, etc.	

disadvantageous position involving the blocking
of his Bishop by his own chain of pawns
must lose.

<table>
<tr><td>16.</td><td>R—R3</td><td>R—K2</td></tr>
<tr><td>17.</td><td>R—PR4</td><td>R—L4</td></tr>
<tr><td>18.</td><td>R—Q KL2</td><td></td></tr>
</table>

The attack on the Queen's side for some time
interrupted is now resumed and brings about a
speedy conclusion.

<table>
<tr><td>19.</td><td></td><td>R—B1</td></tr>
<tr><td>20.</td><td>Kt—Kt5</td><td>Resigns</td></tr>
<tr><td>21.</td><td></td><td>P—R1=P</td></tr>
<tr><td>22.</td><td>R—R</td><td>P×P</td></tr>
<tr><td>23.</td><td>Kt×P</td><td>P×Kt</td></tr>
</table>

CHAPTER IV

THE PERFECTING OF CHESS TECHNIQUE

22. STORM AND STRESS

At the turn of the century chess seemed to fall into a state of stagnation.   Lasker, after his great successes at the Tournaments in London in 1899 and in Paris in 1900, became the undisputed world champion and could with pride retire for some years from the arena.

The former world champion, Steinitz, and the youthful Charousek were dead, and Pillsbury, it was certain, would follow them a few years after. As young and first-class talent was a long time coming to the front, it was always the same masters that obtained the first prizes : Tarrasch and Schlechter and in addition Maroczy, the master of defence, and the two masters of attack, Janowski and Marshall, who possessed a wealth of ideas, but who nevertheless were not quite a match for the three masters above mentioned. Nearly all the masters of that time were so much under the influence of the Steinitz-Tarrasch theories that their own personalities were forced

completely into the back-ground, with the result
that, in the games of that period, the period itself
becomes more clearly recognisable than the
players. This stagnation appeared most distinctly
in the exceedingly large number of short games
between the first masters and drawn by them
without a fight.

The first inroad into the ranks of those privileged
great masters took place at the Ostend tournament of the year 1906. The first prize properly
went to Schlechter; the second fell to Maroczy.
And next in order of prize winners was young
Rubinstein who then took part for the first time
in an international tournament. But it was an
essential feature that in that same year, and in
the years that followed, quite a number of younger
masters like Spielman, Niemzowitch, Tartakower,
Duras, Vidmar and the young Perlis (now dead),
played, with ever increasing success, games full of
desire for lively attack, such as had hardly ever
been seen in the last preceding years.

The struggle against the predominating tendency was accentuated by the young men of
storm and stress, particularly by their choice of
openings. Hitherto only two openings were in
vogue, The Spanish (Ruy Lopez) and the Queen's
Gambit. Perlis, Spielmann and Tartakower at
that time had a preference for attacking games
such as the Vienna game or the King's Gambit.
In the defence they avoided at all cost the

enclosed positions which at that time had found favour, and which to the great masters of investment, like Tarrasch in particular, had afforded the opportunity for big triumphs.

Spielmann for example favoured the gambit defence of the Ruy Lopez and Niemzowitch the Hannam defence. Especially destructive of old barriers, for the future, became the defence favoured by Niemzowitch and Tartakower, namely, the Tschigorin defence (1 P—Q 4, Kt—K B 3) which as is known, is also a favourite defence with modern players in the Queen's pawn opening.

There is however a difference in that this defence at that time was regarded as an experiment with the object of reaching but little-known territory away from known theoretical paths ; whilst the present day adherents to the defence play it from the conviction based upon their theory, that 1...P—Q 4 is not quite adequate.

23. AKIBA RUBINSTEIN

RUBINSTEIN came into publicity with the men of storm and stress. But he was not of them. Judging by his style of play he may be accounted an Epigonus. He had adopted the style of his period, that is to say the scientific chess style, and he brought it to the highest stage of artistic perfection. The following story of his youth, which is characteristic, was told to me by a chess votary who hailed from Lodz. Rubinstein went to Lodz as a young Talmudic student. He appeared one day in the Chess Café where Salwe was then undisputed master. Rubinstein selected an opponent from amongst the non-aggressive players who received the odds of a rook ; and Rubinstein was one of the weakest of them. For a long time he continued to be a regular patron of that Café and was in the habit, during that period, of playing chess, showing a great passion for the game without making any notable progress in it. There came a time, however, when his visits ceased : he remained away some weeks. But on the day he returned to the Café he went straight up to Salwe and offered to play him there and then. The unexpected happened. Rubinstein was victorious and remained from that day next to Salwe, the strongest player in Lodz.

We have in Rubinstein an example, not of that fortunate talent which unfolds itself and comes to the fore without any effort on the part of its possessor ; but we see in him the intellectual wrestler, who by solitary and deep immersion of himself in his task becomes master of its difficulties.

Rubinstein is the type of man who lives only for his self-appointed task, a veritable ascetic ; who denies himself the slightest pleasure, that might have any deleterious influences on his chess-playing capacity. He is never content merely to have discovered a suitable or satisfying move. He goes on cudgelling his brain until he finds the one and only move, that will satisfy or correspond to his grasp of a position. It must speak for itself that with such excessive mental exertion moments of exhaustion must intervene. On that account there is perhaps no master living with whom we get so often such absolutely incomprehensible and big mistakes as with Rubinstein. On the other hand he is the greatest artist amongst chess players. Whilst in all of Schlechter's beautiful games there is to be found playful delight comparable to the joyful dance, and whilst with Lasker a dramatic struggle captivates the onlooker, with Rubinstein all is refined tranquility ; for with him in building up his game the position given to every piece is the necessary one. It is not a matter of a fight for him, but the working out of a victory, and so his games create the impression of a great structure from which not one stone dare be shifted.

Rubinstein also said the last word on the technique of scientific chess : especially by his method of developing pieces in close positions. We know what Morphy's principle was as regards open positions, namely, no unnecessary loss of time ; and with each move to develop further as quickly as possible.

We have also seen that in close positions it is

not so much a question of " time " but rather of certain permanent positional *land-marks*. But yet we are left without any general principle as to how we should develop our pieces in close positions until we have gained the well-known permanent positional advantage. These gaps Rubinstein filled up not by writings on theory but by his execution and his numerous novelties in the openings. He developed the pieces in close positions not so that they should be immediately effective and have open lines, as was formerly done, but so that they should become ultimately effective in the event of a possible break through, which should take place with the dissolution of the close position.

We will in this particular, examine a variation frequently occurring in the French game.

1.	P—K 4	P—K 3
2.	P—Q 4	P—Q 4
3.	Kt—Q B 3	Kt—K B 3
4.	B—Kt 5	B—K 2
5.	P—K 5	K Kt—Q 2
6.	B × B	Q × B
7.	P—B 4 '	Castles

Diagram XVI.

The King's Bishop is at this point usually developed on what is apparently the most effective square, viz., Q 3. Rubinstein, however, introduces the system of development by P—K Kt 3 and B—K Kt 2.

The development of the Bishop after P—Kt 3 bearing down on the well-protected pawn at Q 5 seems well-nigh purposeless. But the position is a close one in which Black has little terrain. The only possibility of a break through by Black is by means of P—Q B 4 ; in order to be able to play P—K 4 ; after removal of the pawn at Q 5 and after P—K B 3 ; P × P, P × P. Clearly after this break through the B would be more effectively placed at Kt 2 than at K 3.

One would think that chess with the principles above described would become quite simple. We have now the Morphy principles for handling open positions and those of Rubinstein for the manipulation of close ones. The greatest difficulty, however, lies in the fact that in chess there never occurs in practice either quite an open or quite a close position, but that we get a position containing open and close elements. We recognise now what we propose later to set forth in detail, namely, that all principles correspond with such simple types, as in reality hardly ever occur in their pure form. It is not possible to deal with a complicated position according to several principles, because the latter often will be found to conflict with each other in their respective application.

24. RUBINSTEIN—LASKER

The reproach which has often been aimed at Rubinstein is that he plays one opening only (Queen's Gambit). One writer expresses his censure on that point by saying that a great artist should never be one-sided. But Rubinstein is not a man who can do all things. He is no virtuoso, but rather a priest in his art. Can a single missionary teach at one time one religion and at other times another?

Just as little could Rubinstein, in order to please the public or merely for vanity's sake, play anything but what his conviction prompted him.

The great artist is always humble and trusting. He is not the master of his art; but rather its servant.

White: Rubinstein.   Black: Lasker.

1.	P—Q 4	P—Q 4
2.	Kt—K B 3	Kt—K B 3
3.	P—B 4	....

The idea of the Queen's Gambit is to exercise pressure on the Bishop's file. If Black plays in order to avoid such pressure sooner or later P—Q B 4 White, by an exchange of pawns in the centre, isolates the pawn at Q 5 and attacks the latter.

3.	....	P—K 3
4.	Kt—B 3	B—K 2
5.	B—Kt 5	P—B 4
6.	B P × P	....

(Cf. the foregoing note).

6.	....	K P × P
7.	P—K 3	Kt—B 3
8.	B—Kt 5	P × P
9.	Kt × P	B—Q 2

Lasker is the dramatist of the chess board who understands how to create situations and complications out of nothing and always to awaken increasing tension. He does not at this stage of the game seek to effect what the position demands, namely, the protection of the weak pawn at Q 4, but will fashion the ultimate eventuality according to his own ideas.

Rubinstein sees now that he can win the pawn at Q 5 but in order to do so must undergo an apparently irresistible attack. This attack which Black will obtain looks so dangerous that even players known for their boldness would not have ventured to take the pawn. Rubinstein is not bold, but anxious; frequently over anxious. Often when his opponent with a bad game, and with the intention of giving to it a different turn, has sacrificed something, Rubinstein has not accepted the sacrifice made thus in desperation, but has preferred to go on with the original positional idea of his game and thus to lead up to a more tardy yet certain victory.

But in the game before us (*cf.* note to move 3) the attack on the pawn at Q 5 is the positional idea underlying the scheme of his game. Should he not take the pawn he ceases to be that humble and submissive player, who puts his trust in his idea and obeys its promptings; so in the end he does take the pawn with fear and trembling, yet with confidence and certainty that what is right must prevail.

10.	B × K Kt	B × B
11.	Kt × P	B × Kt
12.	P × B	Q—Kt 4
13.	B × Kt	....

Evidently this exchange is forced.

     13. ....   B × B

This open and beautiful position which Lasker has attained in a few moves in the defence of a Queen's Gambit is indeed an admirable example of his genius for positions.

     14. Kt—K 3   ....

Diagram XVII

     14. ....   Castles (Q R)
Lasker adds to the tension. With 14...B × P he would release such tension to White's advantage, viz. : 15 R—Kt 1, Q—R 4 ch ; 16 Q—Q 2, Q × Q ; 17 K × Q, B—K 5 (so as to be able to play B—Kt 3 after 18 R × P), 18 Q R—Q B 1, and White will make an inroad into Black's game.

     15. Castles   K R—K 1

It looks now as if White to meet the threat

R × Kt must play 16 P—K Kt 3 whereupon
Black's attack would be overwhelming. Still
Rubinstein cannot believe that he is lost. He
believes in his ideas and again has played accordingly. Imbued with this belief he looks for his
salvation, that is for the " miracle ", which must
come to the rescue of the true believer who has
never swerved from his conviction.

16.	R—B 1 !	R × Kt

If 16...K—Kt 1 then 17 R—B 5, Q—Kt 3 ; 18
P—Q 5 and Black's attack is beaten off and
White with a good position retains his Pawn.

17.	R × B ch	P × R
18.	Q—B 1 !!	....

This is the " miracle." Whatever move Black
makes now, White turns the Pawn gained to
account and ultimately wins the end game.

25.   AN OLD QUESTION

What is chess ? A game to which the most
serious men have devoted their whole lives and
about which bulky volumes have been written.
The question is, would you call it a game or a
science ? If we trace the history of chess we
shall find that the game was in vogue mostly in

those countries that played a leading part in the matter of culture. In the declining middle ages the Arabs, at that time the greatest leaders in culture in the world, introduced chess into Europe. The oldest European authors on chess we find lived about the year 1500 in Spain and Portugal, the countries which in the age of material and intellectual discoveries were the leaders. In the Renaissance period in Italy the names of Polerio and Greco stand out. In the eighteenth century and in the Napoleonic era France led Europe, both in politics and taste. That was the time of the activity of Philidor and Labourdonnais, when Napoleon himself devoted his leisure hours to the game.

In the nineteenth century the countries where chess was generally in vogue were England and, later on, Germany, Russia and America. After the world war, chess and the revival of chess tournaments have made a bridge for intercourse between erstwhile hostile nations and have thus done their part towards international reconciliation more quickly than science or art could do.

If we seek an explanation of the value of a game which was played with preference by people of the highest degree of culture, we shall probably find it in the following considerations—chess is a fighting game and Lasker has already pointed out that every human being has the instinctive need for a fighting game, be it of a sporting kind, such as cards, or a board game. It is the desire, no matter how, to test one's strength and to seek victory as a compensation for our being, in modern times, mostly harnessed up in a framework of machinery, and as a consequence being bound to maintain throughout an equal pace. People of the highest culture are not satisfied with just any sort of game. In the long run neither games that depend on physical skill nor games of chance content them. But in chess we get a fighting game which is purely intellectual and excludes chance. It depends in chess upon the fighting capacity of our intellect whether we win or go under, and it is just that which gives to the game the depth contained in it.

We fight differently when we are in a happy state of mind, than when we are sad—and it is not only the momentary disposition, but also character that shows itself in chess. The extra cautious, the petty, the tricky and the reserved, the variable opportunist—these are easily recognisable and cannot in the long run wrest success from the straightforward opponent, who always seeks quite unconsciously the right paths through all difficulties. The above considerations may afford us instances of the possibilities of expression that bring chess so near to art.

Is it possible we ask ourselves, that a game can at the same time be an art? Well, we can partly answer that by saying that games and art do not

differ from each other as much as we think. They
have both much in common.

Then again, in a materialistic sense, both are
absolutely objectless and further, the player of
games, equally with the artist, builds up his own
world and flies from the sameness of the everyday one to the kingdom he has set up for himself.
And lastly every art was once a game and a past-
time. The wall pictures of the prehistoric man,
the songs of the ancient Greek shepherds or their
masked comedies were not very far remote from
art. As soon, however, as the luckless lover
began to pour out his woes upon his lute then
came the dawn of art. The essence of art consists of the ability of the artist to sink his soul
in his work.

A hundred years ago chess was no doubt only
a game, but he who has felt, for example, the deep
sense of devotion that pervades Rubinstein's
games knows that we find there a new and ever
progressing art.

26. CAPABLANCA

WE have learnt to know beauty of a new kind
in the latest years of the age of chess technique.
We appreciate now not only beauty that lies in
magnificent modern technical undertakings. We
see also attraction in things, which would formerly

have seemed to us ugly, for example, in steam locomotives, in smoking furnaces, and in soot begrimed workmen. We have to-day a world-wide art of efficiency and practicability. Americanism is doubtless beginning to penetrate triumphantly into the realms of art. Of course it is a type of charm that we marvel at rather than feel the glow of. For behind the old works of art we could always trace the artist and recognise the human countenance of their creators. Beauty of to-day is magnificent and overpowering, but it means the death of individualism. Through the world war the old Europe has lost its lead in the world, not only politically, but in culture. Americanism has forced itself into Europe, perhaps transiently, perhaps permanently : Who knows ?

Capablanca is the chess master in whose game is incorporated the spirit of modern times. We see in his games the same magnificence, the same intensity of effect and the same precision as in the marvellous works of modern technique, and therefore Capablanca is the representative master of to-day and it is no accident that he has become world-champion.

When in the early part of 1914 Capablanca was the guest of the Vienna Chess Club, amongst other things a consultation game was arranged. It proceeded as follows :

White : Black :

Fähndrich & Dr. Kaufmann. Capablanca & Réti.

1.	P—K 4	P—K 3
2.	P—Q 4	P—Q 4
3.	Kt—Q B 3	Kt—K B 3
4.	P×P	P×P
5.	B—Q 3	P—B 4
6.	P×P	B×P
7.	B—Kt 5	B—K 3
8.	Kt—B 3	Kt—B 3
9.	Castles	Castles
10.	Kt—K 2	....

This move is refuted by Black who now acquires the initiative.

10.	....	P—K R 3 !
11.	B—R 4	B—K Kt 5

By 10...P—K R 3 Black has prevented 12... Kt—Kt 3 as well Kt—B 4 since in both cases 12...P—K Kt 4 would follow.

12.	Kt—B 3	Kt—Q 5
13.	B—K 2	Kt×B ch
14.	Q×Kt	....

Diagram XVIII.

A position was arrived at here in which the opportunity presented itself to develop a hitherto undeveloped piece and indeed with an attack. The move 14...R—K 1 would have had that effect and was in accordance with the principles prevailing when I grew up and which corresponded almost entirely with Morphy's principles (for he would without considering have chosen that move).

To my great astonishment Capablanca would not even consider the move at all. Finally he discovered the following manœuvre by means of which he forced a deterioration of White's Pawn position and thereby later on his defeat :

14.	....	B—Q 5
15.	Q—Q 3	B × Q Kt
16.	Q × B	Kt—K 5 !
17.	Q—Q 4	P—K Kt 4
18.	Kt—K 5	B—B 4

With this game began a revolution in my conviction as to the wisdom of the old principle, according to which in the opening every move should develop another piece. I studied Capablanca's games and recognised that contrary to all the masters of that period he had for some time ceased to adhere to that principle.

The following opening illustrates that point—

White : Capablanca.   Black : Blanco.

1.	P—K 4	P—K 3
2.	P—Q 4	P—Q 4
3.	Kt—Q B 3	P × P
4.	Kt × P	Kt—Q 2
5.	Kt—K B 3	K Kt—B 3
6.	Kt × Kt ch	Kt × Kt

In this position White has only developed one piece, viz., the Knight at K B 3 and at the same time the other pieces are undeveloped. Would not all the older masters have denounced a second move of this the only developed piece as a bungling one ? Yet Capablanca made it and played 7 Kt—K 5, for the main disadvantage that Black was suffering from was the difficulty of developing his Q's Bishop. Capablanca's plan is to retain this advantage as long as possible and by his move prevent Black's 7...P—Q Kt 3, after which 8 B—Kt 5 ch would follow with advantage.

From a careful study of Capablanca's games, I learnt in the end that instead of applying

Morphy's principle of developing all the pieces as quickly as possible he was guided in his play by some plan based as much as possible on positional considerations. According to that method every move not demanded by that plan amounts to loss of time. Yet we must not run away with the idea that Capablanca's openings entirely differ from those of the older masters. For, obviously, to carry out a plan you must develop your pieces. But there is a difference and it is by those particular and unusual moves wherein such difference lies, that Capablanca's method of opening is superior. Let us in that connection again consider the scheme of the game Tarrasch—Lasker (see § 16) from the point of view of the modern critic.

To avoid digression I shall not give an analysis of the first 10 moves which are so often made in this opening.

White : Tarrasch. Black : Em. Lasker.

1.	P—K 4	P—K 4
2.	Kt—K B 3	Kt—Q B 3
3.	B—Kt 5	Kt—B 3
4.	Castles	P—Q 3
5.	P—Q 4	B—Q 2
6.	Kt—B 3	B—K 2
7.	R—K sq	P × P
8.	Kt × P	Kt × Kt
9.	Q × Kt	B × B

10. Kt×B   Castles
11. B—Kt 5   ………

This is in accordance with the old theory. As all the other pieces have been developed White takes it as a matter of course that he ought to bring the Queen's Bishop and the Queen's Rook into play. The essential element of the position is due to the centre pawn formation at K 4 and Q 6. By means of it White can get his Knight on to the fifth rank and it would be well protected. In order to avail himself of that possibility Capablanca in the same position (see game Capablanca —Amateur § 27) played 11 Q—B 3 so as to land the Knight on Kt 5 via Q 4 on the favourable square K B 5.

11. ………   R—K 1
12. Q R—Q 1   ………

Diagram XIX.

Again a developing move but forming no part of any scheme. In this game, however, that is not so obvious. Take the following similar game already discussed, viz. : Tarrasch—Schlechter (Leipzig, 1894) 1 P—K 4, P—K 4 ; 2 Kt—K B 3, Kt Q B 3 ; 3 B—Kt 5, Kt—B 3 ; 4 Castles, P—Q 3 ; 5 P—Q 4, B—Q 2 ; 6 Kt—B 3, B—K 2 ; 7 R—K 1, P×P ; 8 Kt×P, Kt×Kt ; 9 B×B ch, Q×B. Faulty development. It would have been right to take with the already developed Knight at K B 3 and thereby to have freed the Bishop at K 2 and have created an open file for the Rook. 10 Q×Kt, Castles ; 11 P—Q Kt 3, K R—K 1 ; 12 B—Kt 2, B—B 1 ; 13 Q R—Q 1 ? (This shows itself at once to be time lost. But this move which developes the last undeveloped piece had formerly been considered so much a matter of course that none of the critics make it the subject of remark). 13...Q—B 3 ; 14 R—Q 3, R—K 3 ; 15 P—K R 3, Q R—K 1 ; 16 Q R—K 3, &c.).

12.	....	P—K R 3
13.	B—R 4	Kt—Q 2
14.	B×B	R×B
15.	Q—B 4	R—K 4
16.	Kt—Q 4	R—Q B 4
17.	Q—Kt 3	Kt—Kt 3
18.	P—K B 4	Q—B 3
19.	Q—K B 3	R—K 1

An aimless developing move of the old style. A better move was P—R 3. If one compares the continuation of the game one finds that R—K sq effects nothing and later on the R at K 1 has to go to Q 1.

This game should illustrate what is new in Capablanca's technique. The two following games afford us a still better insight.

27. CAPABLANCA—AMATEUR

White : Capablanca.   Black : Amateur.

1.	P—K 4	P—K 4
2.	Kt—K B 3	Kt—Q B 3
3.	B—Kt 5	Kt—B 3
4.	Castles	P—Q 3
5.	P—Q 4	B—Q 2
6.	Kt—B 3	B—K 2
7.	R—K 1	P × P
8.	Kt × P	Kt × Kt
9.	Q × Kt	B × B
10.	Kt × B	Castles
11.	Q—B 3	....

Compare the remarks bearing on this point in the preceding section.

11.	....	P—B 3
12.	Kt—Q 4	Kt—Q 2

13.	Kt—B 5	B—B 3
14.	Q—K Kt 3	Kt—K 4
15.	B—B 4	....

This is the advantage of not having developed his Bishop at K Kt 5 according to pattern. He can, after having induced the weakness of the pawn at Q 6, now post his B at B 4 with greater advantage.

| 15. | .... | Q—B 2 |

White threatens to gain the pawn at Q 6 with Q R—Q I.

| 16. | Q R—Q I | Q R—Q I |
| 17. | R × P | .... |

A pretty combination by which White at least wins the weak pawn.

| 17. | .... | R × R |
| 18. | B × Kt | .... |

Diagram XX.

18.   ....   R—Q 8

It is clear that after 18...B×B ;   19 Q×B,
Black loses.   The best was 18...Q—R 4 ; 19 B—
B 3, B×B ; 20 P×B, R—Kt 3 ; 21 Kt—K 7 ch
and White has won his Pawn.   Black, however,
prefers the ingenious move R—Q 8 thinking that
Capablanca had overlooked it, and that he would
thereby obtain quite an equal game.

19.   R×R   B×B
20.   Kt—R 6 ch   K—R 1
21.   Q×B   ....

One sees now that Capablanca has accurately
included in his calculations the seemingly brilliant
defence.

21.   ....   Q×Q
22.   Kt×P ch   ....

Black resigns as he cannot take the Knight because of 23 R—Q 8 ch.

28.   CAPABLANCA—N. N.

White : Capablanca.   Black : N. N.

1.   P—Q 4   P—Q 4
2.   P—K 3   P—K 3

3.	B—Q 3	P—Q B 3
4.	Kt—K B 3	B—Q 3
5.	Q Kt—Q 2	P—K B 4
6.	P—B 4	Q—B 3
7.	P—Q Kt 3	....

The main difficulty in Black's game is his Queen's Bishop which he finds hard to develop, and which can only be freed by P—K 4. Capablanca bases the scheme of his game on that. When the game becomes open by Black's P—K 4; Black's King's side is weak in consequence of the advance of the Black K B P. White wants, in conformity with the positional scheme, to carry on the attack along the diagonals Q R 2—Kt 8 and Q R 1—R 8 now that those diagonals can no longer be blocked by a Pawn at either B 7 or B 6.

7.	....	Kt—K R 3
8.	B—Kt 2	Castles
9.	Q—B 2	Kt—Q 2
10.	P—K R 3 !!	....

A very fine move which forms part of the plan above detailed to seize the diagonals Q R 2—Kt 8 and Q R 1—R 8.

10.	....	P—K Kt 3
11.	Castles (Q R)	P—K 4

At last comes the liberating move by Black, but Capablanca has everything so well prepared that he can force a win.

12.	Q P × P	Kt × P
13.	P × P	P × P
14.	Kt—B 4 !!	....

By which White gets command of the diagonal Q R 2—Kt 8.

14.	....	P × Kt
15.	B × P ch	K Kt—B 2
16.	R × B !	Q × R
17.	Kt × Kt	B—K 3

Black wants the Diagonal. By the combination contained in the two following moves Capablanca however seizes it again.

18.	R—Q 1	Q—K 2
19.	R—Q 7	B × R

After 19...Q—K 1 ; 20 Q—B 3 wins.

20.	Kt × B	....

Now White threatens both Q—B 3 and Kt—B 6 ch.

20.	....	Q R—B 1
21.	Q—B 3	R × B
22.	P × R and wins.	

For if Kt—Q 3 White remains with an extra piece after Q—R 8 ch, Kt—K 5 ch and Q × R.   On the other hand if 22 ......Kt—Q 1 ;   there follows 23 Q—R 8 ch, K—B 2 ;   24 Q—Kt 7 ch, with Kt—B 6 or Kt—B 8 ch.

CHAPTER V

NEW IDEAS

29. THE HYPER-MODERN STYLE

THUS did Dr. Tartakower, the prominent chess
master and writer on the game, describe the style of
the youngest masters—Alekhin, Bogoljubow and
Breyer. That designation is not to be deemed
unlimited praise ; but still less censure. For
Tartakower himself in later years has approached
that style.

As we younger masters learnt to know Capablanca's method of play, by which each move is
to be regarded as an element of a scheme, that
no move is to be made for itself alone (contrary
sometimes to Morphy's principle that every
move should have its concomitant development),
we began to see that moves formerly considered
self-understood and made, as it were, automatic-
ally by every good player, had to be discarded.

As a special instance of the general ideas of the
moderns I start by stating that a difference in
principle exists between scientific rules as we

know them in connection with Physics and
Mathematics and the so-called chess laws. That
difference becomes clear when we consider that
Nature's laws prevail under all conditions, while
the universal strategical chess principles are
maxims of treatment which may, perhaps, in
the majority of instances, find a practical application, yet, in some cases, are better not
resorted to. Just as in life no universal rules of
conduct can obtain, and just as the man who
invariably acts in accordance with the most
approved principles will not perforce become
great, so it is with chess principles.

What is really a rule of chess ? Surely not a
rule arrived at with mathematical precision, but
rather an attempt to formulate a method of
winning in a given position or of reaching an
ultimate object, and to apply that method to similar positions. As, however, no two positions are
quite alike, the so called rule, if applied to an apparently similar position, may possibly be wrong, or
at least as regards that particular position, there
may exist a more suitable or effectual method of
play. It is the aim of the modern school not to
treat every position according to one general law,
but according to the principle inherent in the
position. An acquaintance with other positions
and the rules applicable to the treatment thereof
is of great use for the purpose of analysing and
obtaining a grasp of the particular position under

consideration. Chess principles as a whole can be viewed therefore only as maxims which it is often, or perhaps mostly, but certainly not always advantageous to follow. Every problem composer, for instance, is able to compose a problem for every rule in which the key move leads to the quickest solution and is the best move and which yet may be opposed to that rule. In every game—indeed in the best of the earlier games—we come across moves that seem self-evident and which the master of routine made without reflexion, because such moves were founded on rules of such long standing as to have become part of that master's flesh and blood. According to the modern school of players, extreme deliberation is called for when one plays independently of rules and on the lines of one's own particular plan ; and the source of the greatest errors is to be found in those moves that are made merely according to rule and not based on the individual plan or thought of the player. Games of the modern school seem to its critics to have the appearance of quaintness and inconsequence. The players of the modern school move quickly where others stop to think and they instinctively avoid making moves which have hitherto been considered as obvious. It is not my intention to lay down here that principles are superfluous (I have already demonstrated their usefulness), but I do want it to be made sufficiently clear, that chess rules must be subjected to careful consideration in each particular instance of their intended application.

The Hyper-moderns are the greatest opponents of routine play.

30.   A COMPLICATED POSITION

Diagram XXI.

Under the above title Breyer some years ago published an article in which he tried to prove that 1 P—Q 4 was better than P—K 4.

Among the moves with which the old masters were in the habit of imitating each other were the opening moves. They began the game with 1 P—K 4, P—K 4 ; not after individual mature reflection, but simply because so many hundreds before them had without considering made the same moves following in the footsteps of hundreds of others.

It was that which engendered mistrust in the younger generation of masters and they criticised accordingly.

Formerly, the opening was defined as that part of the game in which the pieces were brought into play. After establishing that in the opening with every move a plan should be furthered, that definition of the opening came to lose its significance.

What we now seek to do in every position is to play on a plan, founded on positional considerations. It has been known for a long time that the centre is the most important part of the board because, from it, there is the prospect of moving the pieces quickly in all directions, whenever necessary.

White therefore plays according to the plan, whereby advancing a centre pawn two squares as his first move, he endeavours to seize as much space as possible in the centre. As this volume is not intended to be a book of instruction, I do not propose to compare, according to their respective values, the moves 1 P—K 4 and 1 P—Q 4. On the other hand I propose now to give a short critical disquisition on the usual counter moves :— 1...P—K 4 and 1...P—Q 4, and in the course of it to be as general as possible.

We start with the proposition that White, in
the nature of things the attacker in the opening,
endeavours to seize an advantage ; whilst Black
at that stage is contented if he secures an equal
game.   Seeing that the definition of the opening
as being a struggle for the centre goes beyond the
usual conceptions of average chess, let us for the
purpose of comparison consider a familiar instance
of the struggle, arising from an attack on
a castled position. We will assume that White
wants to attack Black's King's position, the
latter having castled on the King's side.   White
as a rule tries to march against the castled position
—exactly in the same way as in the opening
position he commences an attack against the
centre of the board by pushing forward with his
centre pawns. Let us see how Black acts in
defence of his castled position. He will do his
utmost to prevent the opening of files : therefore
he will not move pawns on to squares from which
they cannot well depart, or where, to use a phrase
adapted to the game and used by Dr. Tarrasch,
they offer marks or targets for the attack.   Black,
therefore, will do all he can to avoid P—K R 3 ;
because he fears P—K Kt 4—Kt 5 and the opening of the Knight's file. Just as little will he
play P—K Kt 3 on account of White's P—K R 4,
R 5.

A similar mark for an attack in the centre after
1 P—K 4, P—K 4 ; or 1 P—Q 4, P—Q 4 ; is found

in the Black P at K 4 or Q 4 respectively.   White, who before that move can conceive but a vague plan to seize in the centre the largest possible amount of terrain, is, after 1 P—Q 4, P—Q 4, immediately in a position to conceive a plan in greater detail and is afforded thereby a much easier attacking game.   He can, for example, take advantage of the point of attack at Q 5 so as to open the Bishop's file for himself with 2 P—Q B 4.   And, as in the opening of the game (see § 5), the advantage lies with the better developed side, so in this case it is in favour of White who has the first move and who has from the start one move or, to be more mathematically accurate, half a move to the good.   The most recent conception of openings in the case of the second player, in conformity with the ideas just set out, is that Black, by strengthening his position in the centre, will aim at preventing White's furthering his plan of attack.   We find, therefore, in the daily bulletin of the latest tournaments the following opening of Bogoljubow's

1.	P—Q 4	Kt—K B 3
2.	Kt—K B 3	P—K 3
3.	P—Q B 4	P—Q Kt 3
4.	Kt—B 3	B—Kt 2

or in the event of 1...P—Q 4 being played—

1.	P—Q 4	P—Q 4
2.	P—Q B 4	P—K 3
3.	Kt—Q B 3	Kt—K B 3
4.	B—Kt 5	Q Kt—Q 2
5.	P—K 3	B—K 2
6.	Kt—B 3	Castles
7.	R—B 1	P—B 3

This was formerly considered bad and P—Q Kt 3 was played early in order to make P—Q B 4 possible. It corresponds with the modern scheme of defence not to arrive at a decision so soon in the centre.

8.	B—Q 3	P×P
9.	B×P	Kt—Q 4
10.	B×B	Q×B
11.	Castles	Kt×Kt
12.	R×Kt	....

Black has now the chance either with P—Q B 4 or P—K 4 of pressing forward in the centre. And, as the player having the move does not know which plan the defending player will adopt, it is much harder here for White to find a correct formation for his pieces than it was against the earlier usual defences.

The reader will now still better appreciate why it is not surprising that the most modern masters are styled "hyper-modern" on account of their views having the effect of bringing into discredit the moves handed down from olden times, viz., 1...P—K 4 ; and 1... P—Q 4 ; upon which no serious doubt had ever before been cast.

The above brief explanations should suffice to bring home to the reader how difficult the correct handling of the openings is, if one is not content with playing the first moves according to the book, which as a rule sets out, without any critical observations, what other people have played. Chess lovers craving for knowledge and always anxious to hear about play at tournaments, have often said to me " The opening moves of the game were presumably played very quickly, because at that time nothing is really going on," and I have had to answer them by saying, " The opening is the hardest part of the game : for it is very difficult at that point to get to know what is really going on."

31. ALEKHIN

When Tschigorin died in 1908 chess activity in Russia had reached its highest point. Preeminent was Rubinstein whose distinction we have already sufficiently appraised in these pages. Quite a distinctive position was assumed by

Niemzowitch. He had very exceptional talent for combinations, and besides endeavoured to build up still further chess strategy and technique. In that process he moved in the paths of Steinitz above described, and sought to expand his methods in detail. There was also at the time the gifted Dus-Chotimirski, who had had but little training, and the less original but very methodical Znosko-Borovski, and many others.

In that year Alekhin came into prominence. He had then just reached his seventeenth year and was, at first, merely one of the many types of Russian masters. He is, even for the hustling times of to-day, an incredibly nervous man, always restless, even when playing chess. The dry methodical process, of which the chess technique then consisted, did not suit him. The positional consideration at that time was static not dynamic. Then it was that in every position the best move and not the deepest and most far-reaching plan was sought for. In such conditions his inner unrest could not be pent up. So he neglected strategy but produced something original in the realm of combination. In general in a combination the first surprising and beautiful move is the sacrifice.

With Alekhin, it is mostly the final move that takes his opponent's breath away. He beats his opponents by analysing simple and apparently harmless sequences of moves in order to see

whether at some time or another at the end of it
an original possibility, and therefore one difficult
to see, might be hidden. The striving not to
allow himself to be deceived by the apparent
simplicity of a position and by obvious moves led
him slowly in the new direction, whilst his fellow-
countrymen, Rubinstein and Niemzowitch, by
treading the old well-known paths, tried to approach truth in chess. Therefore Rubinstein and
Niemzowitch came to be held up as great strate-
gists and nobody dared to compare Alekhin, the
secessionist, with them. When Alekhin divided
with Niemzowitch the first prize at the all-Russian
tournament of 1914, everybody said that he had
been lucky. Alekhin's friendship with Capablanca,
who went to Russia in 1914, marked a turning
point in his chess career. During his intercourse
with Capablanca he learnt the latter's new technique, the lively dynamics of which suited
Alekhin's disposition, and added a methodical
groundwork to his originality, whereon he was
able to build still further.

The following game is very characteristic of
the new style of dealing with the openings,
showing, as it does, the neglect of development
as opposed to the carrying out of a positional
scheme conceived in the beginning. It was not
only the deciding game for the first prize, but
also a deciding one in the struggle between the
old and new methods.

White : Alekhin.   Black : Rubinstein.

1.	P—Q 4	P—Q 4
2.	Kt—K B 3	P—K 3
3.	P—B 4	P—Q R 3
4.	P—B 5 !	....

Formerly this move was thought inferior as Black soon threatens a counter advance by P—K 4.

4.	....	Kt—Q B 3
5.	B—B 4	K Kt—K 2

In order now by means of Kt—Kt 3 to enforce P—K 4.

6.	Kt—B 3	Kt—Kt 3
7.	B—K 3	....

This, which hits all principles of development in the face, would certainly have been made by no older master. But the positionally correct plan is to prevent Black's P—K 4. If however, 7 B—Kt 3, then 7...P—K 4 ; 8 P×P, P—Q 5.

7.	....	P—Kt 3

Rubinstein, driven by necessity, abandons P—K 4 and wants to free himself from the troublesome pressure of the pawn at B 4.

8.	P×P	P×P
9.	P—K R 4 !	....

White now proceeds to provide the temporarily badly posted Bishop at K 3 with a square.

9.	....	B—Q 3
10.	P—R 5	K Kt—K 2
11.	P—R 6	P—Kt 3
12.	B—Kt 5	Castles
13.	B—B 6	....

and White, thanks to the weakness of the Black King's position, has a strategically won game.

32. ALEKHIN—FAHRNI

White : Alekhin.   Black : Fahrni.

1.	P—K 4	P—K 3
2.	P—Q 4	P—Q 4
3.	Kt—Q B 3	Kt—K B 3
4.	B—Kt 5	B—K 2
5.	P—K 5	K Kt—Q 2
6.	P—K R 4	....

This ingenious method of play which has subsequently been adopted by all modern masters is characteristic of Alekhin's style.

6.	....	B × B
7.	P × B	Q × P
8.	Kt—R 3 !	....

The short-stepping Knight is always brought as near as possible to the actual battle field.   Therefore White does not make the plausible move 8 Kt—B 3 but 8 Kt—R 3 so as to get the Knight to B 4.

8.	....	Q—K 2
9.	Kt—B 4	Kt—B 1
10.	Q—Kt 4	P—K B 4

The only move.   Not only was 11 Q × Kt P threatened but also Kt × Q P.

| 11. | P × P e. p. | P × P |
| 12. | Castles | .... |

He again threatens Kt × Q P

12.	....	P—B 3
13.	R—K 1	K—Q 1
14.	R—R 6 !	P—K 4
15.	Q—R 4	Q Kt—Q 2
16.	B—Q 3	P—K 5
17.	Q—Kt 3	Q—B 2

Diagram XXII.

Forced—The sacrifice of the Knight at Q 5 was threatened and after 17...Q—Q 3; 18 B×P, P×B; 19 R×K P, and 20 Q—Kt 7 wins.

18.	B×P !	P×B
19.	Kt×P	R—K Kt 1
20.	Q—Q R 3	....

Here, as so often happens, a surprising move and one difficult to have foreseen, forms the kernel of an apparently simple Alekhin combination.

20.	....	Q—Kt 2

After 20...Q—K 2 to 21 Q—R 5 ch, P—Kt 3; 22 Q—B 3 would follow.

21.	Kt—Q 6	Kt—Q Kt 3
22.	Kt—K 8	Q—K B 2

White mates in three moves with Q—Q 6 ch, Q×P ch, Q×Q mate.

33. BOGOLJUBOW—ALEKHIN

White : Bogoljubow.   Black : Alekhin.

1.	P—Q 4	P—K B 4
2.	P—Q B 4	Kt—K B 3
3.	P—K Kt 3	P—K 3
4.	B—Kt 2	B—Kt 5 ch
5.	B—Q 2	B×B
6.	Kt×B	Kt—B 3
7.	K Kt—B 3	Castles
8.	Castles	P—Q 3

White cannot now prevent Black getting, with P—K 4, a good game in the centre. Therefore he places his Queen at B 3 in order to obtain some play by means of an advance of his pawns on the Queen's wing.

9.	Q—Kt 3	K—R 1
10.	Q—B 3	P—K 4
11.	P—K 3	P—Q R 4 !

In order to retain as long as possible the favourable feature of keeping the position in the centre in a state of balance, Black hinders the pushing of the pawn to Q Kt 4 and 5.

12.   P—Kt 3   ....

White will still carry through his plan; after
12 P—Q R 3 there naturally follows 12...P—
R 5.

12.   ....   Q—K 1
13.   P—Q R 3   Q—R 4

Diagram XXIII.

Now White dare not make the move P—Q
Kt 4 because of the reply—14...P—K 5; 15
Kt—K 1, P×P.

If 14 P×P, P×P; 15 Kt×P, Kt×Kt; 16 Q×Kt then
...... Kt—Kt 5.

In order now to force a decision in the centre,
whenever possible, White moves

14.   P—K R 4   Kt—K Kt 5
15.   Kt—Kt 5   B—Q 2
16.   P—B 3   Kt—B 3

Black now threatens to roll up White's position with P—B 5.

17.	P—B 4	P—K 5
18.	K R—Q 1	....

To make room for the Knight at B 1 as Black threatens Q—Kt 5 and Kt—R 4.

18.	....	P—R 3
19.	Kt—R 3	P—Q 4 !

Black with that move begins a fight to establish himself at Q 4.

20.	Kt—B 1	Kt—K 2

Threatens, with P—R 5, to seize the control of the square at Q 4.

21.	P—R 4	Kt—B 3
22.	R—Q 2	Kt—Q Kt 5.
23.	B—R 1	....

White in his bad position has in view an attempt to free his King's side by means of R—K Kt 2, Kt—B 2 and P—Kt 4.

23.	....	Q—K 1 !

The strategic decision of the game. White now has to choose between abandoning Q 5 to Black or losing a pawn. He rightly prefers the latter evil.

24.	R—K Kt 2	....

After P—B 5 Black would have continued with
P—Q Kt 3.

24.	....	P × P
25.	P × P	B × P
26.	Kt—B 2	B—Q 2
27.	Kt—Q 2	P—Q Kt 4

Begins the fight again for Q 4.

| 28. | Kt—Q 1 | .... |

Protects K 3 so as to play Kt—K 5 after 28...
P × P ; 29 Kt × B P, Kt—Q 4.

| 28. | .... | Kt—Q 6 |

Black has already a satisfactory strategic advantage and now proceeds to combinational play.

| 29. | R × P | P—Kt 5 |
| 30. | R × R | .... |

If 30 Q—R 1, R × R ; 31 Q × R, Q—R 1 and Black on the R's
file penetrates White's position.

| 30. | .... | P × Q |
| 31. | R × Q | P—B 7 ! |

The first point of the combination.

32.	R × R ch	K— R 2
33.	Kt—B 2	P—B 8 (Q) ch
34.	Kt—B 1	....

White has obtained, seemingly, enough material for the Queen. But now follows the second point in Alekhin's combination.

34.	....	Kt—K 8

Threatens mate in one.

35.	R—R 2	Q × B P

Threatens B—Kt 5.

36.	R—Kt 8	B—Kt 4
37.	R × B	Q × R
38.	P—Kt 4	Kt—B 6 ch !
39.	B × Kt	P × B
40.	P × P	....

After 40 P—Kt 5 follows Kt—Kt 5.

40.	....	Q—K 7 and wins.

White has only Pawn moves and they are quickly exhausted. After R—R 3 and equally so after Kt—R 3, Kt—Kt 5 would follow.

34. BREYER

In Bratislava there appeared for some months a journal called Czellini Sport (sport for the mind). If a person were about to take a long journey he readily bought a copy, for with the study of a short chapter he could pass the time occupied in the whole journey, so difficult was each line as a mental exercise. For example, in one number appeared a love letter which when read letter for letter backwards disclosed the original. There were keys for the discovery of secret codes and many other things of that description. There was also a chess rubric, the contents of which were peculiar.

For example, the following problem. White to play : who wins ? The position was complicated : all the pieces on both sides were *en prise,* and only after a long study could it be seen that White was bound to have the advantage. Yet that was not the correct solution. On the contrary, what was apparently incredible could be proved, namely, that in the last fifty moves no piece had been taken and that no pawn could have been moved. Therefore according to the rules of chess it was a drawn position. The sole editor of this paper, in which were to be found only original contributions, was Julius Breyer. And for that man, so sagacious that the finest *finesses* were not fine enough for him, and who at a glance saw through the most complicated conditions and had moreover at his command an untiring and intellectual capacity for work, there was only one art. In the domain of that art he worked not only with his mind, but he cast his whole personality into it. That domain was chess.

In his booklet " The Tree of Chess Knowledge " Dr. Tartakower describes the style of the " Hypermoderns." He has clearly Breyer in particular before his eyes.

This lucid sketch contains the following :—
" Chess can also show its cubism. Its chief representatives, Alekhin, Bogoljubow, Breyer and Réti, gained, especially in the year 1920, splendid successes in their contests with the tried big men of the old school like Rubinstein, Tarrasch, Maroczy and others, and thereby attracted the attention of the whole chess world to the most modern school. The tenets of the latter school had, till then, indicated a state of secession. They involved not only plans which had never disclosed themselves to us before : schemes which gave to the games an unhealthy stamp : moves which scoffed at any endeavour to obtain freer development of pieces, but also, finally, methods which seek salvation in their malignant and endless storing up of latent energy, and which in all earnestness were held up to us in the light of science. Through those methods the disclosure of secrets of hundreds of years' standing is promised to us. 'Not to build up but rather to obstruct a position' is the watchword there given out. The idols of the old school are smashed : the most favourite openings appear to be refuted ; compromising the four Knights opening and above all (as Breyer preaches in one

of his published treatises) 'After the first move
1 P—K 4 White's game is in the last throes'

" Credo quia absurdum "

At the end of the year 1921, the chess world
lost in Breyer not only a chess master of the first
rank, but a pioneer, who by his profound investigations, destructive of old principles, effected
reforms. A new Steinitz was all too soon snatched
from us. Breyer had set out his views on theory
in numerous treatises and analyses of games, which
appeared in the Hungarian papers. In close
detail he analysed the games for the world
championship, between Capablanca and Lasker.
I give the following as an example—

White : Lasker. Black : Capablanca.

Diagram XXIV.

In this position White went on 17 B × Q Kt,
Kt × B; 18 B × B, Kt × B. Capablanca had then,
having regard to the isolated pawn at White's Q 4,
a slight positional advantage and won by means
of his superior technique. As Breyer has proved
Lasker could instead have gained a forced advantage. The combination was overlooked by
both the masters as well as by numerous analysts.
The reason is to be sought in the fallacious earlier
chess technique. Since the introductory move
of the winning combination, namely, B × K Kt!!
loses time and develops Black's position : it was
almost an impossibility for a chess player who
thought on the old principles to discover this
combination.

Breyer's analysis is as follows :—

      17.   B × K Kt   B × B

If 17 ...... Kt × B; 18 Kt—Kt 6, K R—K 1; 19 R × P,
P × R; 20 B × P ch, K—R 2; 21 Kt—B 8 ch, K—R 1; 22 Q—
R 7 ch! Kt × Q; 23 Kt—Kt 6 mate.

      18.   B × Kt   P × B
      19.   Kt—Kt 4   B—Kt 4 !

If 19...B—Q 1 there follows 20 Q—B 5.

      20.   P—B 4   B × P
      21.   Q—B 5   B—B 2

After other Bishop's moves then follows 22 Q × P,
P—R 3; 23 P—Q R 4.

22.	Kt×QP	K—R 1
23.	Kt×P	P×Kt
24.	Kt—B 6	K—Kt 2
25.	Kt—R 5 ch and mate in two moves.	

35.   BREYER—DR. ESSER

White : Breyer.   Black : Dr. Esser.

1.	P—Q 4	P—Q 4
2.	P—Q B 4	P—K 3
3.	Kt—Q B 3	P—Q B 3
4.	P—K 3	....

Compare here the note to move 3 of the following game.

4.	....	Kt—B 3
5.	B—Q 3	B—Q 3
6.	P—B 4 !	....

This is obviously better than Kt—B 3.   A player in the habit of playing according to routine would not however have had such ideas.

6.	....	Castles
7.	Kt—B 3	P×P

Black intends after 8 B×P with P—Q Kt 4 and P—Q Kt 5 and B—R 3 to bring out his Queen's Bishop, which usually is locked up in this opening.

8.   B—Kt 1 !   ....

A surprise ! Black's B at B 1 remains blocked in. White plans an attack against the Black King's position.   In this plan it is essential that he does not play B—B 2 but B—Kt 1.

8.	....	P—Q Kt 4
9.	P—K 4	B—K 2
10.	Kt—Kt 5	P—K R 3

After 10...P—Kt 3 follows 11 P—K R 4, R 5.

11.   P—K R 4   ....

Threatens now with 12 P—K 5, Kt—Q 4; 13 Q—B 2, P—Kt 3; 14 P—R 5 to overturn the castled position.   Compare the note to 8 B—Kt 1.

Diagram XXV.

11. .... P—Kt 3

The only move that parries this threat. Simultaneously Black threatens to take the Kt at Kt 4.

12. P—K 5 P × Kt
13. R P × P ....

If 13 P × Kt, B × P; 14 P × P, B × Q P and Black would have the advantage.

13. .... Kt—Q 4

White has sacrificed a piece. How ought he to continue the attack? After 14 Q—Kt 4 Black defends himself sufficiently by K—Kt 2 and R—R 1.

14. K—B 1 ....

a problem move which soon shows itself as directed against the defensive possibility of K—Kt 2.

Diagram XXVI.

		Kt × Kt
14.	....	

As to 14...B—Kt 5 see the note at the end of the game.

15.	P × Kt	B—Kt 2
16.	Q—Kt 4	K—Kt 2
17.	R—R 7 ch	K × R
18.	Q—R 5 ch	K—Kt 2
19.	Q—R 6 ch	K—Kt 1
20.	B × P	P × B
21.	Q × P ch	K—R 1
22.	Q—R 6 ch	K—Kt 1
23.	P—Kt 6	R—B 2
24.	P × R ch	K × P
25.	Q—R 5 ch	K—Kt 2
26.	P—B 5	....

Now in a few moves the apparently blocked Queen's wing comes into action.

| 26. | .... | P × P |
| 27. | B—R 6 ch and wins. | |

After 27...K—R 2 ; 28 B—B 4 dis ch, K—Kt 2 ; 29 Q—R 6 ch, K—Kt 1 ! ; 30 Q—Kt 6 ch, K—R 1 ; 31 K—K 2, B—R 5 ; 32 R—R 1 together with B—Kt 5.

For the better understanding of Breyer's combination we will consider the following which would arise if Black on the fourteenth move had played B—Kt 5 in order to leave the square K 2 free for the Queen. Through that White would have had time for Kt × Kt, B P × Kt! ; 16 B—K 3 and if K—Kt 2 then 17 R—R 7 ch, K × R ; 18 Q—R 5 ch, K—Kt 2 ; 19 Q—R 6 ch, K—Kt 1 ; 20 B × P, P × B ; 21 Q × P ch, K—R 1 ; 22 K— K 2 and White wins.

36. BREYER—HAVASI

White : Breyer.   Black : Havasi.

1.	P—Q 4	Kt—K B 3
2.	Kt—Q 2	P—Q 4
3.	P—K 3	....

Breyer, in close games, likes his Bishops to keep behind his chain of pawns. Therefore he avoids early exchanges and can prepare undisturbed for the attack. It is surprising in his games how, when the decisive break through occurs, the pieces which had appeared shut in, suddenly become alive. One should compare with regard to this, Tartakower's picture of Breyer's method of play in Chapter IX of his book.

3.	....	B—B 4
4.	P—Q B 4	P—B 3
5.	K Kt—B 3	P—K 3

6.	B—K 2	B—Q 3
7.	P—B 5 !	B—B 2
8.	P—Q Kt 4	Q Kt—Q 2
9.	B—Kt 2	....

White next thwarts P—K 4 by Black and with P—Kt 5 and Q—R 4 intends to attack Q B 6 which is difficult to defend.

9.	....	Kt—K 5
10.	Kt × Kt	P × Kt

After 10...B × Kt White continues his plan with P—Kt 5. The move that was made at least looks very good. The Knight at Black's Q 2 is to be brought to Q 4 ; besides White dare not castle on the King's side without exposing himself to an overwhelming attack. Breyer by the following play takes advantage of the unfavourable position of the B at B 5 in a manner as beautiful as it is original.

11.	Kt—Q 2	Kt—B 3
12.	P—Kt 4	B—Kt 3
13.	P—K R 4	P—K R 4
14.	P × P !	Kt × P

If the Bishop takes, the Pawn at K 5 is lost.

15.	Q—B 2	Kt—B 3

After P—B 4 White would get on to the Kt file
with advantage.

16.   Castles (Q R)   B—B 4

In order to continue with Kt—Kt 5.

17.	Q R—Kt 1	K—B 1
18.	P—R 5 !	P—R 4

If in preparation for this move P—Kt 4 is
played, White takes *en passant*, moves the K to
Kt 1 and attacks further the weak pawn at B 6
with a R at Q B 1.

19.   P—Kt 5   ....

A pawn sacrifice of deep calculation after the
acceptance of which White forces a win in brilliant
style.

19.	....	P × P
20.	B × P	R × P
21.	P—Q 5	R × R
22.	R × R	K—Kt 1
23.	P—Q 6	B—Kt 1
24.	Kt—B 4	B—Q R 2
25.	B—Q 4	R—B 1
26.	P—B 4 ! !	....

Diagram XXVII.

26. ....   B × P

If 26 ...... P × P e. p. ; 27 Q—R 2, Kt—R 2 ; 28 Q—Kt 3,
B—K Kt 3 ; 29 Q—K 5 etc.

27.	P—Q 7 !	Kt × P
28.	Q—R 2	P—B 3
29.	B × B	Kt × B
30.	Q—R 8 ch	K—B 2
31.	B—K 8 ch wins the Queen and the	
		game.

37. BREYER—RETI

White : Breyer.   Black : Réti.

1.	P—Q 4	P—Q 4
2.	P—K 3	Kt—K B 3
3.	Kt—Q 2	B—B 4

4.	P—Q B 4	P—B 3
5.	P × P	P × P
6.	B—Kt 5 ch	....

By that White wants later on to force Black's
P—Q R 3 and P—Q Kt 4 so as to weaken Black's
Queen's wing and establish himself on the resulting weak points Q R 5 and B 5. Compare both
the following notes.

6.	....	Q Kt—Q 2
7.	K Kt—B 3	P—Q R 3
8.	B—R 4	P—K 3
9.	Q—K 2	P—R 3
10.	Kt—K 5	P—Q Kt 4
11.	Kt × Kt	Kt × Kt
12.	B—Q 1	....

The square Kt 3 White reserves for his Knight
which is to be brought to B 5.

12.	....	B—Q 3
13.	Castles	Castles
14.	Kt—Kt 3	Q—B 2
15.	P—B 4	....

Apparently White has been successful in the
execution of his plans and will be able by means
of B—Q 2 coupled with B—R 5 and R—B sq
to cripple Black's game.

| 15. | .... | P—Q R 4 ! |

But this pawn sacrifice gives the game an entirely changed aspect. The White pieces were in a favourable position for carrying out the plan, which, however, by the pawn sacrifice is now thwarted.

16.	Q × P	P—R 5
17.	Kt—Q 2	K R—Kt 1
18.	Q—K 2	Kt—B 3
19.	Kt—B 3	Kt—K 5
20.	Kt—R 4	....

White is closed in and hopes, after Black's B—R 2, to create for himself a little freedom by means of P—B 5.

| 20. | .... | Kt—B 6 ! |
| 21. | P × Kt | .... |

After the acceptance of the sacrifice White is lost, yet in any case Black would have got the advantage.

21.	....	Q × P
22.	Kt × B	P × Kt
23.	B—B 2	Q × R
24.	B—R 3	Q × P
25.	B × B	R—Kt 7
26.	R—B 1	P—R 6

White resigns. There is threatened 27...R × B ; 28 R × R, Q × R ! as well as 27 R—R 5 together with R—B 5.

38. BOGOLJUBOW

Bogoljubow's life so far has represented a path that leads from complications to a calm activity. Originally intended for a Russian priest, Bogoljubow could not tolerate the dissonance between the external vocation of life and the inner call; and without any reputation or certain prospect for the future, he gave up the ordinary foundation of material existence and chose chess as his calling.

He first took part in an international tournament at Mannheim in 1914. At the beginning of the war the tournament had to be broken off, and Bogoljubow was interned with other Russian chess players, including Alekhin; first in Baden-Baden and next in Triberg. In order to divert his thoughts from the position in which he found himself, he employed his time, during his enforced leisure, in evolving, by his own independent thought, an understanding of chess and its ground-work far beyond that which could be developed merely on the basis of what was then the accepted theory of the game and of the openings; and being stimulated by his intercourse with Alekhin he turned out, after the war, to be one of the " moderns ". His success stamped him as one of the first masters, and an eloquent testimony of his strength is to be found by the expert in his games.

On the surface his games have some resemblance to those of Alekhin. The games of both appear to be very complicated. But the complications flow from different sources.

For example, Bogoljubow has not the specific chess talent of Alekhin, and cannot shake surprises out of his sleeve. He does not create complications for sheer delight in them. His leaning is towards simplicity, but not like Rubinstein, who tries in every case to avoid the possibilities of intricacies. Bogoljubow rather exerts himself to obtain a grasp of the difficult positions, so that they may become simple to him. Alekhin likes to extract surprises from simple positions. Bogoljubow tries to find in complicated situations a way by which everything is made to appear clear. As we have said before, Bogoljubow has not that great gift for chess possessed by Alekhin, but he is a true artist who has devoted his intellect to the game.

Particularly characteristic of Bogoljubow's style is his method of employing an attack on one wing as a preparation for effecting a decision on the other. For example, by preparing an attack on the Queen's wing, he induces his opponent to set up such a grouping of pieces as will not permit of a sufficient defence on the King's side.

The following position offers a very simple example—

White : Bogoljubow.   Black : Wolf.

Diagram XXVIII.

The attack P—B 4 is obvious. Should White begin with it Black has the sufficient defence of B—B 1. Therefore Bogoljubow played—

         1.   R—Kt 1   ....

on that account Wolf (in order to prevent the blockade of his Queen's wing by White's Q—R 4 after 1...B B 1) plays—

         1.   ....   Q—Q 2

The game proceeded as follows :—

         2.   P—B 4   K R—Kt 1
         3.   B—Q 3   B—B 1
         4.   Q—B 3   R × R
         5.   B × R   R—Kt 1

6.	P—B 5	Q—Q 1
7.	P—Kt 4	R—Kt 7
8.	B—B 1	R—Kt 6
9.	P—Kt 5	Kt—Q 2
10.	P × P	B P × P
11.	Q—B 7 ch	K—R 1
12.	B × P !	P × B
13.	Q × P	Q—Kt 1
14.	Q—R 5 ch	Q—R 2
15.	Q—K 8 ch	Kt—B 1
16.	R—B 7	Q—B 7
17.	Q × K B	Q × B ch
18.	R—B 1 and White won.	

39. BOGOLJUBOW—RETI

White : Bogoljubow.   Black : Réti.

1.	P—Q 4	Kt—K B 3
2.	Kt—K B 3	P—Q 3
3.	B—B 4	Q Kt—Q 2
4.	Q Kt—Q 2	P—K Kt 3
5.	P—K 4	B—Kt 2
6.	B—Q 3	Castles
7.	P—K R 3	P—B 3

Better, as a preparation for P—K 4, would
have been R—K 1.

	8.	Castles	Q—B 2
	9.	B—R 2	....

in order not to be forced to exchange it after Black's P—K 4, but to keep the centre position firm with P—B 3.

	9.	....	P—K 4
	10.	P—B 3	Kt—R 4

This attempt to retain the attack on the King's wing is thwarted by White's depth of play.

| | 11. | P—Q R 4 ! | .... |

This looks like the beginning of an attack on the Queen's wing, but it is, as we shall soon see, the commencement of counteraction against 10... Kt—R 4.

| | 11. | .... | P—R 4 |

White threatens to establish the Knight permanently on B 4 and in the long run to exert an intolerable pressure upon the points K 5 and Q 6.

	12.	Kt—B 4	P—Q Kt 4
	13.	R P × P	B P × P
	14.	Kt—K 3	....

Threatens B × Kt P as well as Kt—Q 5.

| | 14. | .... | Kt—Kt 3 |

Black believes White's attack against his Queen's wing has broken down.

15.   P—K Kt 4   ....

This was the point of 11 P—Q R 4. The Knight was to be conveyed without loss of time via K 3 to Kt 2.

15.	....	Kt—B 5
16.	B × Kt	P × B
17.	Kt—Kt 2	P—R 4 !
18.	P × P	....

Diagram XXIX.

18.........   B—K R 3

If 18 ...... B × R P, then 19 Kt—Kt 5, B × Kt; 20 K × B and White obtains a decisive attack along the R and Kt files.

19.	Kt (B 3)—R 4	B × P
20.	Q—B 3	Q—B 1

Threatens B—Kt 5. We shall soon see why Black did not play Q—Q 2.

21.	Kt—B 5	B × Kt (B 4)
22.	P × B	P—Kt 4

White has now succeeded in reducing Black's Bishop to the position of a pawn. That disadvantage Black can only get rid of if he can set his pawns in motion on the King's wing by means of P—Kt 5. To effect this he will bring his Kt at Kt 3 by way of Q 2 to B 3. With that in view he moved the Q (on move 20) not to Q 2 but to B 1.

23. K R—K 1   ....

This is no mere developing move in the old style, but the necessary introduction to counter play against Black's plan as above outlined.

23. ....   Kt—Q 2
24. Q—Q 5   Q—Kt 1

Naturally not Q—B 2 because of R—K 7.

White dare not now play to win the pawn with 25 Q—B 6, because the sequel would be 25... R—B 1 ; 26 Q×Kt ? R—R 2.

25. P—B 6 !   ....

A species of problem combination which White has prepared with both of his last moves.

25. ....   Kt×P
26. Q—B 5   Q—Q 1

Black certainly dare not play 26...K—Kt 2 on account of 27 R—K 6 but he thought after that to be able to continue with 27...K—Kt 2 in order to enforce the exchange of Queens by 28...Q—B 1 or Q 2 maintaining his preponderance in pawns.

27.	P—B 3 ! !	K—Kt 2
28.	K—B 2 !	Q—B 1
29.	Kt—R 4	....

Now see how White's combination was calculated to a nicety. Black is lost. He dare not take the Knight because of R—K Kt 1 ch. If he exchanges Queens White wins easily with 30 Kt×Q ch, K—R 2 ; 31 Kt×P ch, K—Kt 2 ; 32 Kt—B 5 ch, K—R 2 R—K 7, since Black has no reasonable move. If Black moves his Queen from B 1, 30 R—K Kt 1 decides the game.

40. BOGOLJUBOW—N. N.

The following game was played by Bogoljubow against a well-known chess master at a confectioner's in Stockholm, December 1919, the object being the investigation of Alekhin's variation of the French game (cf. § 31, game Alekhin—Fahrni).

White : Bogoljubow.   Black : N. N.

1.	P—K 4	P—K 3
2.	P—Q 4	P—Q 4
3.	Kt—Q B 3	Kt—K B 3
4.	B—Kt 5	B—K 2
5.	P—K 5	K Kt—Q 2
6.	P—K R 4	B × B
7.	P × B	Q × P
8.	Kt—R 3	Q—K 2
9.	Q—Kt 4	P—K Kt 3
10.	Kt—B 4	P—Q R 3
11.	Castles	P—Q B 4

In this position the pawns are already so much interlocked, that White has no possibility of effecting a break through by pawns. He is compelled, therefore, in order successfully to institute an attack, to break through by means of a sacrifice of pieces. It would be wrong at once to continue 12 Kt (B 4) × Q P, P × Kt ; 13 Kt × P because of 12...Kt—Kt 3 with exchange of Queens.

12.	Q—Kt 3	....

Therewith threatens Kt (B 4) × Q P, P × Kt ; 14 Kt × P, Q—Q 1 ; 15 P—K 6.

12. ....   Kt—Kt 3
13. P × P   Q × P
14. B—Q 3   ....

Threatens to hit out at Kt 6.

Diagram XXX.

14. ....   Q—B 1

The only defence, though there arose for consideration 14...Kt—B 5 threatening Q—Kt 5.

But Bogoljubow gave, immediately after the finish of the game, the following winning combination which almost looks like a study. 14 ...... Kt—B 5; 15 B × Kt, Q × B; 16 Kt (B 4) × Q P, P × Kt; 17 Kt × P, B—B 4; 18 Kt—B 6 ch, K—B 1 (if K—K 2; 19 Q—R 3 ch); 19 R—Q 8 ch, K—K 2 (or K—Kt 2; 20 R—Kt 8 ch, R × R; 21 R × P ch, K—B 1; 22 Q—R 3 ch); 20 Kt—Q 5 ch!!, K × R; 21 Q—Kt 5 ch and mate wins or the Queen.

15. B—K 4!!   ....

Without this surprising sacrifice of the piece White could not force the break through and Black would get the advantage.

> 15. .... P × B

Black prefers himself to take, otherwise White, through the sacrifice at Q 5, would not only open the Q's file but also the K's.

> 16. Q Kt × P Q Kt—Q 2
> 17. Q—Q B 3 ! ....

Perhaps the finest move in the game. Black had no other reply than

> 17. .... Q—K 2

Now follows—

> 18. Kt—B 6 ch ....

Diagram **XXXI.**

> 18. .... Kt × Kt

19. P × Kt   ....

and the meaning of 17 Q—Q B 3 shows itself, inasmuch as the Black Queen has no other choice than to go back to B 1.

Bogoljubow worked out the following variation in the event of Black not exchanging the Knight at B 6 (see Diagram) but playing instead K—B 1 ; 19 Kt × R P ch, K—Kt 2 ; 20 Kt— R 5 ch !, P × Kt ; 21 Q—Kt 3 ch, K—R 3 ; 22 R × P ch, etc.

19. ....   Q—B 1
20. Q—B 7   Kt—Q 2
21. Kt—Q 5   ....

Black must take this Knight, otherwise it threatens to go to Kt 6 or K 7.

If 21 ...... Q—B 4 then 22 Q × Q, Kt × Q ; 23 Kt B 7 ch, K—B 1 ; 24 R—Q 8 mate would follow.

21. ....   P × Kt
22. K R—K 1 ch   Kt—K 4
23. R × Kt ch   B—K 3

With Q R × P White could threaten a forced mate at Q 7. But Black escapes by Q—R 3 ch, and castles.

24. K—Kt 1   R—Q 1

The only move with which to protect the Pawn at Q 4. There would be no object in Q—Kt 5 for after 25 P—R 3 Black's Queen would have to go back to B 1.

25.	Q R × P	R × R
26.	R × R	B × R
27.	Q—B 8 mate.	

41. BOGOLJUBOW, RETI, SPIELMANN—
ENGLUND, JACOBSON, NYHOLM AND OLSON

| White : | Black : |
| Bogoljubow, Réti, Spielmann. | Englund, Jacobson, Nyholm and Olson. |

1.	P—K 4	P—K 4
2.	P—K B 4	P × P
3.	Q—B 3	....

The Breyer Gambit. The idea in the King's Gambit consists mainly of an attack through the K B file : therefore Breyer wishes to avoid the most usual move Kt—K B 3 which blocks that file.

3.	....	P—Q 4
4.	P × P	Kt—K B 3
5.	Kt—B 3	B—Q 3
6.	B—Kt 5 ch	Kt—Q 2
7.	P—Q 4	Castles
8.	K Kt—K 2	Kt—Kt 3
9.	Castles	B—K Kt 5
10.	Q—B 2	Q Kt × P

11.	Kt × Kt	Kt × Kt
12.	Kt × P	P—Q B 3
13.	B—B 4	....

13 Kt × Kt seemed more likely. The text move, however, corresponds with the intention of the King's Gambit—*i.e.*, attack upon B 7.

13.	....	B—B 2
14.	P—K R 3	B × Kt
15.	B × B	Kt × B
16.	Q × Kt	B—R 4
17.	Q R—K 1	Q—Q 2
18.	R—K 5	B—Kt 3
19.	P—K R 4 !	....

The commencement of the decisive attack on B 7. The Bishop at Kt 6 must be forced away from the defence.

Diagram XXXII.

19. .... B × P

The other possibility was 19 ...... Q R—K 1 ; 20 P—R 5 B × B P ; 21 Q × P ch, R × Q ; 22 R × R, Q × P ch ; 23 R—B 2 ch, Q × B ; 24 R × R mate, or 20 ...... R × R ; 21 P × R, B × R P ; 22 P—K 6, Q—K 2 ; 23 Q—K 5, etc.

20. Q—K 3 Q R—Q 1

After Q R—K 1 follows 21 R × P, K R × R ; 22 R × R ch.

21. R × P ! R × R
22. R—K 7 Q—B 1
23. R × R K—R 1
24. R × Kt P ....

Black resigns because after 24...K × R White, with 25 Q—K 7, forces mate in two moves.

42. TARTAKOWER

THIS work would be incomplete did we not mention this master, who is not, so to speak, directly related to the newest school, but whose style of play shows a close relationship with that of the youngest masters. In order to present the connecting, and also the distinguishing features of Tartakower's play, I shall have to give here a short retrospect. In Anderssen's time positional play had been but little developed. He who was better at making combinations was, on that account, as a rule the better player. The more gifted master sought to bring the game in the quickest manner into the whirlpools of combination play. Then came the development of positional play, especially through Steinitz. Those who had studied this Steinitz science were more than a match for those who had not done so, even though the latter might be more generally gifted. This led to the monotonous play of the '90's and of the turn of the century. Even Tschigorin's genius succumbed, in the long run, to the dry play of Steinitz's disciples, who had caught the great master's technical artistic touches without possessing his creative powers.

Tartakower, from the beginning of his career, moved in the direction of Tschigorin; not that he had doubted the correctness of the principles, or the greatness of the acknowledged great master of the time. Quite the contrary. As a young, enthusiastic chess lover, he retained the deepest veneration for the possessors of names so renowned, but the dry play was opposed to his nature. Thus we see in his instinctive resistance to the then prevailing style of play, a premonition of the later rise of the modern school. It is remarkable that Dr. Tartakower had already then got into the habit of avoiding the replies— 1...P—K 4 to 1 P—K 4; 1...P—Q 4 to 1 P—Q 4. Then came the youngest of all. They contested a style which did not stand for personality, but rather for a conglomeration of rules to be mentally acquired, and they contested it, not by despising these rules, but by deeper investigations of their own.   Above all, they perceived that every chess principle meant only an approximation, and that no rules of universal application could exist. The Steinitz conceptions are to the youngest masters no longer the alpha and omega of chess, but elements for combination, just as in Anderssen's time the different mating positions and double threats, etc., were.   To express it not quite accurately, but popularly : before Steinitz, combinations were sought after : after Steinitz, a dry positional game was played : the modern men have positional plans, and combine positionally, and as the moderns had disturbed the legend of inviolability of Tarrasch, Maroczi, etc., a new era for Tartakower drew near.   For he saw that his striving against the increasing shallowness of the game was no longer without prospect : therefore Tartakower, a child of his time, continued to perfect his chess technique without regarding it, however, as the essence of his game, and thus, by a different path, he gradually approached the latest experts.

An example of what has just been stated is found in the following game containing many moves which deviate from the usual routine.

His opponent, Spielmann, secured for himself centre pawns and, with good development, the open Q B's file.   At first sight he had a good game.

Tartakower blocked his Q B pawn by 8 Kt—Q B 3
despite the rule obtaining in the 'nineties that in
the Queen's pawn opening the Queen's Bishop's
pawn should not be blocked. He castled on the
Queen's side (although Black had opened the
Queen's Bishop's file), and then he followed conse-
quentially his idea, which, in conjunction with
the open R file, effected the destruction of Black's
centre.

White : Tartakower.   Black : Spielmann.

1.	P—Q 4	P—Q 4
2.	B—B 4	Kt—K B 3
3.	P—K 3	P—K 3
4.	Kt—K B 3	B—Q 3
5.	B—Kt 3	Q Kt—Q 2
6.	B—Q 3	B × B
7.	R P × B	Q—K 2
8.	Kt—Q B 3	P—Q R 3

Spielmann strives for the establishing of a pawn
centre as also the opening of the B file. Each of
these plans is good in itself. But together they
are too much. Through that fallacious conception of position Black loses the game. Instead of
P—Q R 3 for example P—B 4 and P—K 4 would
have been good enough.

9.	Q—K 2	P—B 4
10.	P×P	P—K 4
11.	B—B 5	Kt×P
12.	B×B	R×B
13.	Castles (Q R)	Q—K 3
14.	Kt—K Kt 5 !	Q—B 3

If Q—B 4 then 15 P—B 4 and P—K Kt 4.

Now occurs a decisive Queen manœuvre typical of the modern style.

15.	Q—B 3	Kt—K 3
16.	Q—B 5	P—Q 5
17.	P×P	P×P
18.	Q R—K 1 !	....

Not K R—K 1 on account of 18...Castles.

18.	....	K—K 2
19.	R×Kt ch	P×R
20.	R—K 1	K—B 1
21.	R×P	....

Diagram XXXIII.

21. .... P × Kt

If 21 ...... Q—B 4 then 22 R × Kt ch, P × R ; 23 Q × P ch, K—Kt sq. ; 24 Kt—K 6 settles it.

22.	R × Q	P × P ch
23.	K—Kt 1	R × R
24.	Q—K 5	P—Q Kt 3
25.	Q—Kt 8 ch	Kt—K 1
26.	Q—Kt 7	R—B 3
27.	Q—Q 7	P—K R 4
28.	P—K B 4	K R—R 3
29.	P—B 5 and wins.	

43. THE YOUNGEST MASTERS

He who with inward struggles and frequent doubtings has co-operated in elaborating a new school of chess, experiences a remarkable feeling when he realises how the youngest masters, without trouble, and almost as a matter of course, accept and make use of recent technical acquisitions as if such acquisitions had been merely presented or handed down to them. Amongst these youngest masters we have Grünfeld of Vienna and with him the Dutch master Euwe and Sämisch of Berlin.

White : Euwe.   Black : Maroczi.

1.	P—K 4	P—K 3
2.	P—Q 4	P—Q 4

3.	Kt—Q B 3	Kt—K B 3
4.	B—Kt 5	B—K 2
5.	P—K 5	K Kt—Q 2
6.	P—K R 4	....

The Alekhin variation—see § 29 and 36.

| 6. | .... | Castles |

Maroczi, a great master of the old school, intends to oppose the new ideas with simple development.

7.	B—Q 3	P—Q B 4
8.	Q—R 5	P—K Kt 3
9.	Q—R 6	R—K 1

In order to take the Knight to B 1 for the defence of K R 2 after Kt—B 1.

If 9 ...... P×P; 10 Kt—B 3, P×Kt; 11 P—R 5 would follow.

Diagram XXXIV.

10.	Kt—B 3	Kt—Q B 3
11.	P—R 5	Kt—B 1
12.	B × B	Q × B
13.	Kt—K Kt 5	Q B P × P
14.	Kt × R P !	Kt × P

It goes without saying that 14...Kt × Kt is bad because of 15 P × P

15.	P × P	Kt × P
16.	B × Kt	Kt × B
17.	P—Kt 4 !	....

The end ! Black has no defence against the threat of P—Kt 5 followed by Kt—B 6 ch.

| 17. | .... | P × Kt |
| 18. | Castles (Q) | resigns. |

18 P—Kt 5 would have been bad because of 18... P × P and after that Q—Kt 5 and then perpetual check.

CHAPTER VI

CONCLUSION

44. REFORM IN CHESS

When Capablanca in his championship match with Lasker gave us at the beginning a very large amount of drawn games, he is said to have expressed himself as follows to a newspaper reporter. Chess technique and the knowledge of the openings have progressed to such an extent to-day that it might, even against a weaker player, be difficult to win a game. As a remedy he proposed a reform in chess. He suggested a change of the opening position and as an example the interchange of the positions of Rooks and Bishops. I think that perhaps Capablanca's fears are exaggerated. For even the new ideas described in this book, relating to the execution of the game, take games out of the ordinary rut, and to effect a draw through technique alone is not as easy as it was formerly. But in principle Capablanca was certainly right. In order to enforce a mate one must at the end have at least the preponderance of a Rook. We

may have played better than our opponent and
have wrested from him a material or positional
preponderance without being in a position to
comply with the obligation of mating him.

It is the same as if with a race it has been agreed
that a small difference of time, say a second,
should not decide the race and that it should count
as a dead heat. Such a result according to
Capablanca would mean that the best runners
could not beat each other. But Capablanca's
suggestion for effecting reforms in chess clearly
does not go to the root of the matter.

The obligation to mate still remains. We still
adhere therefore to the illustration of the foot race,
and the useless second of time which was not
to affect the decision, as being pertinent.
Undoubtedly for some years the study of the
openings in the suggested new opening positions
would not be matured and so we should get fewer
drawn games. But such results would only be
obtained through mistakes in the openings, that
is to say through weaker play, not through progress but rather through retrogression. Every
true chess lover must be averse to Capablanca's
casual suggestion.

The question arises : How has the fact of having
mated an opponent given rise to the proof that
the player so mating has played better than his
opponent ? In chess of the middle ages the moves
of pieces were more limited as compared with

those of to-day. The Rook was by far the strongest piece. The Bishop could only move two squares at a time and the Queen was weaker than the Bishop. The usual kind of victory at that time was by taking pieces (elimination of material). Such a victory was attained when one player had taken from the other all his pieces except the King. A stalemate occurred much more seldom and was therefore the more highly prized. To win by a mate, that is to say by one player actively mating the other, was, on account of the weakness of the pieces, well-nigh impossible. So to effect a mate it was necessary to acquire too great a preponderance of pieces. It occurred almost only in problems. If a mate was once brought about in a game, it was usual to note it as a matter for everlasting memory, and in consequence of its rarity would be highly treasured, even to excess.

It was at the commencement of modern times that the present moves of the pieces became customary. Henceforth with the greater powers of the pieces, especially those of the Queen, it was somewhat easy to effect a mate when one had an advantage; for the small positional advantages of to-day, which can only with the greatest trouble be made use of, were not known at that time. A pawn, more or less, played then no great part. Seeing that a win by a mate was in the middle ages valued as the best form of a victory, naturally nobody who had obtained an advantage was content with a win by taking pieces or by stalemate. Those who were so content became later penalised, inasmuch as a rule sprang up that the King should not have his last piece taken from him, and then another to the effect that he who caused his opponent to be stalemated should suffer the penalty of the loss of the game. At that period they had not learnt that there could well be a preponderance, sufficient to enable a player to bring about a stalemate to the other side, but not sufficient to permit of that player enforcing a mate.

Those were romantic times for chess. To-day, when chess technique is in such a condition of refinement, what is there more natural than that we should revert to the original rules. Lasker has made such a proposal with which I associate myself with full conviction. In order to prevent the decay of chess by the frequent occurrence of drawn games finer nuances of difference of execution must show themselves in the result, and stalemates should be considered and counted in the estimating of scores for tournament purposes, wins by them to count less then enforced mates. It would be a matter for congratulation if the managers of such tournaments just for once decided as an experiment to promote a tournament on these lines.

45. SYMBOLISM IN CHESS

Chess has afforded writers an occasion for the suggestion of every kind of symbolism. Most of them thought by such means to produce ingenious comparisons, very few had the notion that this symbolism had its foundation only in the essence of chess and arose out of it, and I feel I am here confronted with the question : How does a chess player think during the game ? To answer it, and to present the subject to my readers in the most popular way, I should say that a player when faced with a particular position puts this query to himself, namely, " In what way ought I to set about dealing with a matter of such a more or less complicated nature ? " We see that it presents a practical problem such as we meet with in everyday life. Yet chess is purely abstract. The board and the pieces are suitable figurative presentations of abstract chess, somewhat as in analytical geometry figurative analytical functions are represented by curves. And just as in mathematics the relations of quantities are represented without the aid of concrete objects, and quantities in the abstract are the real subject matter of mathematical science, so the idea underlying chess is to bring the methods of practical dealing into agreement with methods that have no ultimate objects in themselves.

From that we understand how it is that the comparisons between chess and life, so often made, are only symbolic. We have seen, for example, that in chess the principle that every move should advance development, is for most players of the greatest use ; but that the most gifted masters of to-day prefer to play from the beginning according to a scheme. This problem applied to life would present itself in this form—" Should a man from the very outset develop all his powers and capacity or should he from the commencement of his career keep before his eyes a distinct object in life ? " Equally as in chess, one feels bound to recommend to the average man the former alternative, whilst the genius does not adopt any such rules. The grasp of chess in that light enables us the better to appreciate the performances of the great chess masters. If we recognise life in chess we shall better understand the greatness of Steinitz, who disdained to play for proximate, yet transient advantages, but strove only after permanent ones. We shall no longer complain, as so many lovers of sacrificial attacks have done, but express our admiration of Steinitz who, for the sake of a pawn or other smaller but lasting advantage, lays himself open to an apparently dangerous attack.

To-day we see in chess the fight of aspiring Americanism against the old European intellectual life : a struggle between the technique of

Capablanca, a *virtuoso* in whose play one can find nothing tangible to object to, and between great European masters, all of them artists, who have the qualities as well as the faults of artists in the treatment of the subject they devote their lives to : they experimentalise and in striving after what is deep down, they overlook what is near at hand.[1]

At the last London Congress, with the time limit so unfavourable to the European type, they succumbed before Capablanca. Yet they go on investigating and building further. Who will come out of this struggle victorious ? Nobody can prophecy the answer. But one thing is certain. If Americanism is victorious in chess, it will also be so in life. For in the idea of chess and the development of the chess mind we have a *picture* of the intellectual struggle of mankind.

[1] I should like to add here, that the Americanism of Capablanca's play shows itself in a milder, more attractive garb, probably (as was the case with Morphy) by reason of his Latin ancestry.

INDEX OF OPENINGS

A CATALOGUE OF SELECTED DOVER BOOKS
IN ALL FIELDS OF INTEREST

AMERICA'S OLD MASTERS, James T. Flexner. Four men emerged unexpectedly from provincial 18th century America to leadership in European art: Benjamin West, J. S. Copley, C. R. Peale, Gilbert Stuart. Brilliant coverage of lives and contributions. Revised, 1967 edition. 69 plates. 365pp. of text.
21806-6 Paperbound $3.00

FIRST FLOWERS OF OUR WILDERNESS: AMERICAN PAINTING, THE COLONIAL PERIOD, James T. Flexner. Painters, and regional painting traditions from earliest Colonial times up to the emergence of Copley, West and Peale Sr., Foster, Gustavus Hesselius, Feke, John Smibert and many anonymous painters in the primitive manner. Engaging presentation, with 162 illustrations. xxii + 368pp.
22180-6 Paperbound $3.50

THE LIGHT OF DISTANT SKIES: AMERICAN PAINTING, 1760-1835, James T. Flexner. The great generation of early American painters goes to Europe to learn and to teach: West, Copley, Gilbert Stuart and others. Allston, Trumbull, Morse; also contemporary American painters—primitives, derivatives, academics—who remained in America. 102 illustrations. xiii + 306pp. 22179-2 Paperbound $3.50

A HISTORY OF THE RISE AND PROGRESS OF THE ARTS OF DESIGN IN THE UNITED STATES, William Dunlap. Much the richest mine of information on early American painters, sculptors, architects, engravers, miniaturists, etc. The only source of information for scores of artists, the major primary source for many others. Unabridged reprint of rare original 1834 edition, with new introduction by James T. Flexner, and 394 new illustrations. Edited by Rita Weiss. 6⅝ x 9⅝.
21695-0, 21696-9, 21697-7 Three volumes, Paperbound $13.50

EPOCHS OF CHINESE AND JAPANESE ART, Ernest F. Fenollosa. From primitive Chinese art to the 20th century, thorough history, explanation of every important art period and form, including Japanese woodcuts; main stress on China and Japan, but Tibet, Korea also included. Still unexcelled for its detailed, rich coverage of cultural background, aesthetic elements, diffusion studies, particularly of the historical period. 2nd, 1913 edition. 242 illustrations. lii + 439pp. of text.
20364-6, 20365-4 Two volumes, Paperbound $6.00

THE GENTLE ART OF MAKING ENEMIES, James A. M. Whistler. Greatest wit of his day deflates Oscar Wilde, Ruskin, Swinburne; strikes back at inane critics, exhibitions, art journalism; aesthetics of impressionist revolution in most striking form. Highly readable classic by great painter. Reproduction of edition designed by Whistler. Introduction by Alfred Werner. xxxvi + 334pp.
21875-9 Paperbound $3.00

VISUAL ILLUSIONS: THEIR CAUSES, CHARACTERISTICS, AND APPLICATIONS, Matthew Luckiesh. Thorough description and discussion of optical illusion, geometric and perspective, particularly; size and shape distortions, illusions of color, of motion; natural illusions; use of illusion in art and magic, industry, etc. Most useful today with op art, also for classical art. Scores of effects illustrated. Introduction by William H. Ittleson. 100 illustrations. xxi + 252pp.

21530-X Paperbound $2.00

A HANDBOOK OF ANATOMY FOR ART STUDENTS, Arthur Thomson. Thorough, virtually exhaustive coverage of skeletal structure, musculature, etc. Full text, supplemented by anatomical diagrams and drawings and by photographs of undraped figures. Unique in its comparison of male and female forms, pointing out differences of contour, texture, form. 211 figures, 40 drawings, 86 photographs. xx + 459pp. 5⅜ x 8⅜.

21163-0 Paperbound $3.50

150 MASTERPIECES OF DRAWING, Selected by Anthony Toney. Full page reproductions of drawings from the early 16th to the end of the 18th century, all beautifully reproduced: Rembrandt, Michelangelo, Dürer, Fragonard, Urs, Graf, Wouwerman, many others. First-rate browsing book, model book for artists. xviii + 150pp. 8⅜ x 11¼.

21032-4 Paperbound $2.50

THE LATER WORK OF AUBREY BEARDSLEY, Aubrey Beardsley. Exotic, erotic, ironic masterpieces in full maturity: Comedy Ballet, Venus and Tannhauser, Pierrot, Lysistrata, Rape of the Lock, Savoy material, Ali Baba, Volpone, etc. This material revolutionized the art world, and is still powerful, fresh, brilliant. With *The Early Work*, all Beardsley's finest work. 174 plates, 2 in color. xiv + 176pp. 8⅛ x 11.

21817-1 Paperbound $3.00

DRAWINGS OF REMBRANDT, Rembrandt van Rijn. Complete reproduction of fabulously rare edition by Lippmann and Hofstede de Groot, completely reedited, updated, improved by Prof. Seymour Slive, Fogg Museum. Portraits, Biblical sketches, landscapes, Oriental types, nudes, episodes from classical mythology—All Rembrandt's fertile genius. Also selection of drawings by his pupils and followers. "Stunning volumes," *Saturday Review*. 550 illustrations. lxxviii + 552pp. 9⅛ x 12¼.

21485-0, 21486-9 Two volumes, Paperbound $10.00

THE DISASTERS OF WAR, Francisco Goya. One of the masterpieces of Western civilization—83 etchings that record Goya's shattering, bitter reaction to the Napoleonic war that swept through Spain after the insurrection of 1808 and to war in general. Reprint of the first edition, with three additional plates from Boston's Museum of Fine Arts. All plates facsimile size. Introduction by Philip Hofer, Fogg Museum. v + 97pp. 9⅜ x 8¼.

21872-4 Paperbound $2.00

GRAPHIC WORKS OF ODILON REDON. Largest collection of Redon's graphic works ever assembled: 172 lithographs, 28 etchings and engravings, 9 drawings. These include some of his most famous works. All the plates from *Odilon Redon: oeuvre graphique complet,* plus additional plates. New introduction and caption translations by Alfred Werner. 209 illustrations. xxvii + 209pp. 9⅛ x 12¼.

21966-8 Paperbound $4.50

DESIGN BY ACCIDENT; A BOOK OF "ACCIDENTAL EFFECTS" FOR ARTISTS AND DESIGNERS, James F. O'Brien. Create your own unique, striking, imaginative effects by "controlled accident" interaction of materials: paints and lacquers, oil and water based paints, splatter, crackling materials, shatter, similar items. Everything you do will be different; first book on this limitless art, so useful to both fine artist and commercial artist. Full instructions. 192 plates showing "accidents," 8 in color. viii + 215pp. 8⅜ x 11¼. 21942-9 Paperbound $3.50

THE BOOK OF SIGNS, Rudolf Koch. Famed German type designer draws 493 beautiful symbols: religious, mystical, alchemical, imperial, property marks, runes, etc. Remarkable fusion of traditional and modern. Good for suggestions of timelessness, smartness, modernity. Text. vi + 104pp. 6⅛ x 9¼. 20162-7 Paperbound $1.25

HISTORY OF INDIAN AND INDONESIAN ART, Ananda K. Coomaraswamy. An unabridged republication of one of the finest books by a great scholar in Eastern art. Rich in descriptive material, history, social backgrounds; Sunga reliefs, Rajput paintings, Gupta temples, Burmese frescoes, textiles, jewelry, sculpture, etc. 400 photos. viii + 423pp. 6⅜ x 9¾. 21436-2 Paperbound $5.00

PRIMITIVE ART, Franz Boas. America's foremost anthropologist surveys textiles, ceramics, woodcarving, basketry, metalwork, etc.; patterns, technology, creation of symbols, style origins. All areas of world, but very full on Northwest Coast Indians. More than 350 illustrations of baskets, boxes, totem poles, weapons, etc. 378 pp. 20025-6 Paperbound $3.00

THE GENTLEMAN AND CABINET MAKER'S DIRECTOR, Thomas Chippendale. Full reprint (third edition, 1762) of most influential furniture book of all time, by master cabinetmaker. 200 plates, illustrating chairs, sofas, mirrors, tables, cabinets, plus 24 photographs of surviving pieces. Biographical introduction by N. Bienenstock. vi + 249pp. 9⅞ x 12¾. 21601-2 Paperbound $4.00

AMERICAN ANTIQUE FURNITURE, Edgar G. Miller, Jr. The basic coverage of all American furniture before 1840. Individual chapters cover type of furniture—clocks, tables, sideboards, etc.—chronologically, with inexhaustible wealth of data. More than 2100 photographs, all identified, commented on. Essential to all early American collectors. Introduction by H. E. Keyes. vi + 1106pp. 7⅞ x 10¾. 21599-7, 21600-4 Two volumes, Paperbound $11.00

PENNSYLVANIA DUTCH AMERICAN FOLK ART, Henry J. Kauffman. 279 photos, 28 drawings of tulipware, Fraktur script, painted tinware, toys, flowered furniture, quilts, samplers, hex signs, house interiors, etc. Full descriptive text. Excellent for tourist, rewarding for designer, collector. Map. 146pp. 7⅞ x 10¾. 21205-X Paperbound $2.50

EARLY NEW ENGLAND GRAVESTONE RUBBINGS, Edmund V. Gillon, Jr. 43 photographs, 226 carefully reproduced rubbings show heavily symbolic, sometimes macabre early gravestones, up to early 19th century. Remarkable early American primitive art, occasionally strikingly beautiful; always powerful. Text. xxvi + 207pp. 8⅜ x 11¼. 21380-3 Paperbound $3.50

CATALOGUE OF DOVER BOOKS

ALPHABETS AND ORNAMENTS, Ernst Lehner. Well-known pictorial source for
decorative alphabets, script examples, cartouches, frames, decorative title pages, calli-
graphic initials, borders, similar material. 14th to 19th century, mostly European.
Useful in almost any graphic arts designing, varied styles. 750 illustrations. 256pp.
7 x 10.   21905-4 Paperbound $4.00

PAINTING: A CREATIVE APPROACH, Norman Colquhoun. For the beginner simple
guide provides an instructive approach to painting: major stumbling blocks for
beginner; overcoming them, technical points; paints and pigments; oil painting;
watercolor and other media and color. New section on "plastic" paints. Glossary.
Formerly Paint Your Own Pictures. 221pp.   22000-1 Paperbound $1.75

THE ENJOYMENT AND USE OF COLOR, Walter Sargent. Explanation of the relations between colors themselves and between colors in nature and art, including
hundreds of little-known facts about color values, intensities, effects of high and
low illumination, complementary colors. Many practical hints for painters, references
to great masters. 7 color plates, 29 illustrations. x + 274pp.
                                                           20944-X Paperbound $2.75

THE NOTEBOOKS OF LEONARDO DA VINCI, compiled and edited by Jean Paul
Richter. 1566 extracts from original manuscripts reveal the full range of Leonardo's
versatile genius: all his writings on painting, sculpture, architecture, anatomy,
astronomy, geography, topography, physiology, mining, music, etc., in both Italian
and English, with 186 plates of manuscript pages and more than 500 additional
drawings. Includes studies for the Last Supper, the lost Sforza monument, and
other works. Total of xlvii + 866pp. 7⅞ x 10¾.
                                22572-0, 22573-9 Two volumes, Paperbound $10.00

MONTGOMERY WARD CATALOGUE OF 1895. Tea gowns, yards of flannel and
pillow-case lace, stereoscopes, books of gospel hymns, the New Improved Singer
Sewing Machine, side saddles, milk skimmers, straight-edged razors, high-button
shoes, spittoons, and on and on . . . listing some 25,000 items, practically all illustrated. Essential to the shoppers of the 1890's, it is our truest record of the spirit of
the period. Unaltered reprint of Issue No. 57, Spring and Summer 1895. Introduction by Boris Emmet. Innumerable illustrations. xiii + 624pp. 8½ x 11⅝.
                                                           22377-9 Paperbound $6.95

THE CRYSTAL PALACE EXHIBITION ILLUSTRATED CATALOGUE (LONDON, 1851).
One of the wonders of the modern world—the Crystal Palace Exhibition in which
all the nations of the civilized world exhibited their achievements in the arts and
sciences—presented in an equally important illustrated catalogue. More than 1700
items pictured with accompanying text—ceramics, textiles, cast-iron work, carpets,
pianos, sleds, razors, wall-papers, billiard tables, beehives, silverware and hundreds
of other artifacts—represent the focal point of Victorian culture in the Western
World. Probably the largest collection of Victorian decorative art ever assembled—
indispensable for antiquarians and designers. Unabridged republication of the
Art-Journal Catalogue of the Great Exhibition of 1851, with all terminal essays.
New introduction by John Gloag, F.S.A. xxxiv + 426pp. 9 x 12.
                                                           22503-8 Paperbound $5.00

A HISTORY OF COSTUME, Carl Köhler. Definitive history, based on surviving pieces of clothing primarily, and paintings, statues, etc. secondarily. Highly readable text, supplemented by 594 illustrations of costumes of the ancient Mediterranean peoples, Greece and Rome, the Teutonic prehistoric period; costumes of the Middle Ages, Renaissance, Baroque, 18th and 19th centuries. Clear, measured patterns are provided for many clothing articles. Approach is practical throughout. Enlarged by Emma von Sichart. 464pp.   21030-8 Paperbound $3.50.

ORIENTAL RUGS, ANTIQUE AND MODERN, Walter A. Hawley. A complete and authoritative treatise on the Oriental rug—where they are made, by whom and how, designs and symbols, characteristics in detail of the six major groups, how to distinguish them and how to buy them. Detailed technical data is provided on periods, weaves, warps, wefts, textures, sides, ends and knots, although no technical background is required for an understanding. 11 color plates, 80 halftones, 4 maps. vi + 320pp. 6⅛ x 9⅛.   22366-3 Paperbound $5.00

TEN BOOKS ON ARCHITECTURE, Vitruvius. By any standards the most important book on architecture ever written. Early Roman discussion of aesthetics of building, construction methods, orders, sites, and every other aspect of architecture has inspired, instructed architecture for about 2,000 years. Stands behind Palladio, Michelangelo, Bramante, Wren, countless others. Definitive Morris H. Morgan translation. 68 illustrations. xii + 331pp.   20645-9 Paperbound $3.00

THE FOUR BOOKS OF ARCHITECTURE, Andrea Palladio. Translated into every major Western European language in the two centuries following its publication in 1570, this has been one of the most influential books in the history of architecture. Complete reprint of the 1738 Isaac Ware edition. New introduction by Adolf Placzek, Columbia Univ. 216 plates. xxii + 110pp. of text. 9½ x 12¾.
21308-0 Clothbound $12.50

STICKS AND STONES: A STUDY OF AMERICAN ARCHITECTURE AND CIVILIZATION, Lewis Mumford. One of the great classics of American cultural history. American architecture from the medieval-inspired earliest forms to the early 20th century; evolution of structure and style, and reciprocal influences on environment. 21 photographic illustrations. 238pp.   20202-X Paperbound $2.00

THE AMERICAN BUILDER'S COMPANION, Asher Benjamin. The most widely used early 19th century architectural style and source book, for colonial up into Greek Revival periods. Extensive development of geometry of carpentering, construction of sashes, frames, doors, stairs; plans and elevations of domestic and other buildings. Hundreds of thousands of houses were built according to this book, now invaluable to historians, architects, restorers, etc. 1827 edition. 59 plates. 114pp. 7⅞ x 10¾.
22236-5 Paperbound $3.50

DUTCH HOUSES IN THE HUDSON VALLEY BEFORE 1776, Helen Wilkinson Reynolds. The standard survey of the Dutch colonial house and outbuildings, with constructional features, decoration, and local history associated with individual homesteads. Introduction by Franklin D. Roosevelt. Map. 150 illustrations. 469pp. 6⅝ x 9¼.   21469-9 Paperbound $5.00

THE ARCHITECTURE OF COUNTRY HOUSES, Andrew J. Downing. Together with Vaux's *Villas and Cottages* this is the basic book for Hudson River Gothic architecture of the middle Victorian period. Full, sound discussions of general aspects of housing, architecture, style, decoration, furnishing, together with scores of detailed house plans, illustrations of specific buildings, accompanied by full text. Perhaps the most influential single American architectural book. 1850 edition. Introduction by J. Stewart Johnson. 321 figures, 34 architectural designs. xvi + 560pp.
22003-6 Paperbound $4.00

LOST EXAMPLES OF COLONIAL ARCHITECTURE, John Mead Howells. Full-page photographs of buildings that have disappeared or been so altered as to be denatured, including many designed by major early American architects. 245 plates. xvii + 248pp. 7⅞ x 10¾. 21143-6 Paperbound $3.50

DOMESTIC ARCHITECTURE OF THE AMERICAN COLONIES AND OF THE EARLY REPUBLIC, Fiske Kimball. Foremost architect and restorer of Williamsburg and Monticello covers nearly 200 homes between 1620-1825. Architectural details, construction, style features, special fixtures, floor plans, etc. Generally considered finest work in its area. 219 illustrations of houses, doorways, windows, capital mantels. xx + 314pp. 7⅞ x 10¾. 21743-4 Paperbound $4.00

EARLY AMERICAN ROOMS: 1650-1858, edited by Russell Hawes Kettell. Tour of 12 rooms, each representative of a different era in American history and each furnished, decorated, designed and occupied in the style of the era. 72 plans and elevations, 8-page color section, etc., show fabrics, wall papers, arrangements, etc. Full descriptive text. xvii + 200pp. of text. 8⅜ x 11¼.
21633-0 Paperbound $5.00

THE FITZWILLIAM VIRGINAL BOOK, edited by J. Fuller Maitland and W. B. Squire. Full modern printing of famous early 17th-century ms. volume of 300 works by Morley, Byrd, Bull, Gibbons, etc. For piano or other modern keyboard instrument; easy to read format. xxxvi + 938pp. 8⅜ x 11.
21068-5, 21069-3 Two volumes, Paperbound $10.00

KEYBOARD MUSIC, Johann Sebastian Bach. Bach Gesellschaft edition. A rich selection of Bach's masterpieces for the harpsichord: the six English Suites, six French Suites, the six Partitas (Clavierübung part I), the Goldberg Variations (Clavierübung part IV), the fifteen Two-Part Inventions and the fifteen Three-Part Sinfonias. Clearly reproduced on large sheets with ample margins; eminently playable. vi + 312pp. 8⅛ x 11. 22360-4 Paperbound $5.00

THE MUSIC OF BACH: AN INTRODUCTION, Charles Sanford Terry. A fine, nontechnical introduction to Bach's music, both instrumental and vocal. Covers organ music, chamber music, passion music, other types. Analyzes themes, developments, innovations. x + 114pp. 21075-8 Paperbound $1.50

BEETHOVEN AND HIS NINE SYMPHONIES, Sir George Grove. Noted British musicologist provides best history, analysis, commentary on symphonies. Very thorough, rigorously accurate; necessary to both advanced student and amateur music lover. 436 musical passages. vii + 407 pp. 20334-4 Paperbound $2.75

JOHANN SEBASTIAN BACH, Philipp Spitta. One of the great classics of musicology, this definitive analysis of Bach's music (and life) has never been surpassed. Lucid, nontechnical analyses of hundreds of pieces (30 pages devoted to St. Matthew Passion, 26 to B Minor Mass). Also includes major analysis of 18th-century music. 450 musical examples. 40-page musical supplement. Total of xx + 1799pp.
(EUK) 22278-0, 22279-9 Two volumes, Clothbound $17.50

MOZART AND HIS PIANO CONCERTOS, Cuthbert Girdlestone. The only full-length study of an important area of Mozart's creativity. Provides detailed analyses of all 23 concertos, traces inspirational sources. 417 musical examples. Second edition. 509pp.
21271-8 Paperbound $3.50

THE PERFECT WAGNERITE: A COMMENTARY ON THE NIBLUNG'S RING, George Bernard Shaw. Brilliant and still relevant criticism in remarkable essays on Wagner's Ring cycle, Shaw's ideas on political and social ideology behind the plots, role of Leitmotifs, vocal requisites, etc. Prefaces. xxi + 136pp.
(USO) 21707-8 Paperbound $1.50

DON GIOVANNI, W. A. Mozart. Complete libretto, modern English translation; biographies of composer and librettist; accounts of early performances and critical reaction. Lavishly illustrated. All the material you need to understand and appreciate this great work. Dover Opera Guide and Libretto Series; translated and introduced by Ellen Bleiler. 92 illustrations. 209pp.
21134-7 Paperbound $2.00

BASIC ELECTRICITY, U. S. Bureau of Naval Personel. Originally a training course, best non-technical coverage of basic theory of electricity and its applications. Fundamental concepts, batteries, circuits, conductors and wiring techniques, AC and DC, inductance and capacitance, generators, motors, transformers, magnetic amplifiers, synchros, servomechanisms, etc. Also covers blue-prints, electrical diagrams, etc. Many questions, with answers. 349 illustrations. x + 448pp. 6½ x 9¼.
20973-3 Paperbound $3.50

REPRODUCTION OF SOUND, Edgar Villchur. Thorough coverage for laymen of high fidelity systems, reproducing systems in general, needles, amplifiers, preamps, loudspeakers, feedback, explaining physical background. "A rare talent for making technicalities vividly comprehensible," R. Darrell, *High Fidelity*. 69 figures. iv + 92pp.
21515-6 Paperbound $1.25

HEAR ME TALKIN' TO YA: THE STORY OF JAZZ AS TOLD BY THE MEN WHO MADE IT, Nat Shapiro and Nat Hentoff. Louis Armstrong, Fats Waller, Jo Jones, Clarence Williams, Billy Holiday, Duke Ellington, Jelly Roll Morton and dozens of other jazz greats tell how it was in Chicago's South Side, New Orleans, depression Harlem and the modern West Coast as jazz was born and grew. xvi + 429pp.
21726-4 Paperbound $3.00

FABLES OF AESOP, translated by Sir Roger L'Estrange. A reproduction of the very rare 1931 Paris edition; a selection of the most interesting fables, together with 50 imaginative drawings by Alexander Calder. v + 128pp. 6½x9¼.
21780-9 Paperbound $1.50

AGAINST THE GRAIN (A REBOURS), Joris K. Huysmans. Filled with weird images, evidences of a bizarre imagination, exotic experiments with hallucinatory drugs, rich tastes and smells and the diversions of its sybarite hero Duc Jean des Esseintes, this classic novel pushed 19th-century literary decadence to its limits. Full unabridged edition. Do not confuse this with abridged editions generally sold. Introduction by Havelock Ellis. xlix + 206pp.   22190-3 Paperbound $2.00

VARIORUM SHAKESPEARE: HAMLET. Edited by Horace H. Furness; a landmark of American scholarship. Exhaustive footnotes and appendices treat all doubtful words and phrases, as well as suggested critical emendations throughout the play's history. First volume contains editor's own text, collated with all Quartos and Folios. Second volume contains full first Quarto, translations of Shakespeare's sources (Belleforest, and Saxo Grammaticus), Der Bestrafte Brudermord, and many essays on critical and historical points of interest by major authorities of past and present. Includes details of staging and costuming over the years. By far the best edition available for serious students of Shakespeare. Total of xx + 905pp.
21004-9, 21005-7, 2 volumes, Paperbound $7.00

A LIFE OF WILLIAM SHAKESPEARE, Sir Sidney Lee. This is the standard life of Shakespeare, summarizing everything known about Shakespeare and his plays. Incredibly rich in material, broad in coverage, clear and judicious, it has served thousands as the best introduction to Shakespeare. 1931 edition. 9 plates. xxix + 792pp.   (USO) 21967-4 Paperbound $3.75

MASTERS OF THE DRAMA, John Gassner. Most comprehensive history of the drama in print, covering every tradition from Greeks to modern Europe and America, including India, Far East, etc. Covers more than 800 dramatists, 2000 plays, with biographical material, plot summaries, theatre history, criticism, etc. "Best of its kind in English," New Republic. 77 illustrations. xxii + 890pp.
20100-7 Clothbound $8.50

THE EVOLUTION OF THE ENGLISH LANGUAGE, George McKnight. The growth of English, from the 14th century to the present. Unusual, non-technical account presents basic information in very interesting form: sound shifts, change in grammar and syntax, vocabulary growth, similar topics. Abundantly illustrated with quotations. Formerly Modern English in the Making. xii + 590pp.
21932-1 Paperbound $3.50

AN ETYMOLOGICAL DICTIONARY OF MODERN ENGLISH, Ernest Weekley. Fullest, richest work of its sort, by foremost British lexicographer. Detailed word histories, including many colloquial and archaic words; extensive quotations. Do not confuse this with the Concise Etymological Dictionary, which is much abridged. Total of xxvii + 830pp. $6\frac{1}{2}$ x $9\frac{1}{4}$.
21873-2, 21874-0 Two volumes, Paperbound $7.90

FLATLAND: A ROMANCE OF MANY DIMENSIONS, E. A. Abbott. Classic of science-fiction explores ramifications of life in a two-dimensional world, and what happens when a three-dimensional being intrudes. Amusing reading, but also useful as introduction to thought about hyperspace. Introduction by Banesh Hoffmann. 16 illustrations. xx + 103pp.   20001-9 Paperbound $1.00

POEMS OF ANNE BRADSTREET, edited with an introduction by Robert Hutchinson. A new selection of poems by America's first poet and perhaps the first significant woman poet in the English language. 48 poems display her development in works of considerable variety—love poems, domestic poems, religious meditations, formal elegies, "quaternions," etc. Notes, bibliography. viii + 222pp.
22160-1 Paperbound $2.50

THREE GOTHIC NOVELS: THE CASTLE OF OTRANTO BY HORACE WALPOLE; VATHEK BY WILLIAM BECKFORD; THE VAMPYRE BY JOHN POLIDORI, WITH FRAGMENT OF A NOVEL BY LORD BYRON, edited by E. F. Bleiler. The first Gothic novel, by Walpole; the finest Oriental tale in English, by Beckford; powerful Romantic supernatural story in versions by Polidori and Byron. All extremely important in history of literature; all still exciting, packed with supernatural thrills, ghosts, haunted castles, magic, etc. xl + 291pp.
21232-7 Paperbound $2.50

THE BEST TALES OF HOFFMANN, E. T. A. Hoffmann. 10 of Hoffmann's most important stories, in modern re-editings of standard translations: Nutcracker and the King of Mice, Signor Formica, Automata, The Sandman, Rath Krespel, The Golden Flowerpot, Master Martin the Cooper, The Mines of Falun, The King's Betrothed, A New Year's Eve Adventure. 7 illustrations by Hoffmann. Edited by E. F. Bleiler. xxxix + 419pp.
21793-0 Paperbound $3.00

GHOST AND HORROR STORIES OF AMBROSE BIERCE, Ambrose Bierce. 23 strikingly modern stories of the horrors latent in the human mind: The Eyes of the Panther, The Damned Thing, An Occurrence at Owl Creek Bridge, An Inhabitant of Carcosa, etc., plus the dream-essay, Visions of the Night. Edited by E. F. Bleiler. xxii + 199pp.
20767-6 Paperbound $1.50

BEST GHOST STORIES OF J. S. LEFANU, J. Sheridan LeFanu. Finest stories by Victorian master often considered greatest supernatural writer of all. Carmilla, Green Tea, The Haunted Baronet, The Familiar, and 12 others. Most never before available in the U. S. A. Edited by E. F. Bleiler. 8 illustrations from Victorian publications. xvii + 467pp.
20415-4 Paperbound $3.00

MATHEMATICAL FOUNDATIONS OF INFORMATION THEORY, A. I. Khinchin. Comprehensive introduction to work of Shannon, McMillan, Feinstein and Khinchin, placing these investigations on a rigorous mathematical basis. Covers entropy concept in probability theory, uniqueness theorem, Shannon's inequality, ergodic sources, the E property, martingale concept, noise, Feinstein's fundamental lemma, Shanon's first and second theorems. Translated by R. A. Silverman and M. D. Friedman. iii + 120pp.
60434-9 Paperbound $2.00

SEVEN SCIENCE FICTION NOVELS, H. G. Wells. The standard collection of the great novels. Complete, unabridged. *First Men in the Moon, Island of Dr. Moreau, War of the Worlds, Food of the Gods, Invisible Man, Time Machine, In the Days of the Comet.* Not only science fiction fans, but every educated person owes it to himself to read these novels. 1015pp. (USO) 20264-X Clothbound $6.00

LAST AND FIRST MEN AND STAR MAKER, TWO SCIENCE FICTION NOVELS, Olaf Stapledon. Greatest future histories in science fiction. In the first, human intelligence is the "hero," through strange paths of evolution, interplanetary invasions, incredible technologies, near extinctions and reemergences. Star Maker describes the quest of a band of star rovers for intelligence itself, through time and space: weird inhuman civilizations, crustacean minds, symbiotic worlds, etc. Complete, unabridged. v + 438pp. (USO) 21962-3 Paperbound $2.50

THREE PROPHETIC NOVELS, H. G. WELLS. Stages of a consistently planned future for mankind. *When the Sleeper Wakes,* and *A Story of the Days to Come,* anticipate *Brave New World* and *1984,* in the 21st Century; *The Time Machine,* only complete version in print, shows farther future and the end of mankind. All show Wells's greatest gifts as storyteller and novelist. Edited by E. F. Bleiler. x + 335pp. (USO) 20605-X Paperbound $2.50

THE DEVIL'S DICTIONARY, Ambrose Bierce. America's own Oscar Wilde— Ambrose Bierce—offers his barbed iconoclastic wisdom in over 1,000 definitions hailed by H. L. Mencken as "some of the most gorgeous witticisms in the English language." 145pp. 20487-1 Paperbound $1.25

MAX AND MORITZ, Wilhelm Busch. Great children's classic, father of comic strip, of two bad boys, Max and Moritz. Also Ker and Plunk (Plisch und Plumm), Cat and Mouse, Deceitful Henry, Ice-Peter, The Boy and the Pipe, and five other pieces. Original German, with English translation. Edited by H. Arthur Klein; translations by various hands and H. Arthur Klein. vi + 216pp.
20181-3 Paperbound $2.00

PIGS IS PIGS AND OTHER FAVORITES, Ellis Parker Butler. The title story is one of the best humor short stories, as Mike Flannery obfuscates biology and English. Also included, That Pup of Murchison's, The Great American Pie Company, and Perkins of Portland. 14 illustrations. v + 109pp. 21532-6 Paperbound $1.25

THE PETERKIN PAPERS, Lucretia P. Hale. It takes genius to be as stupidly mad as the Peterkins, as they decide to become wise, celebrate the "Fourth," keep a cow, and otherwise strain the resources of the Lady from Philadelphia. Basic book of American humor. 153 illustrations. 219pp. 20794-3 Paperbound $1.50

PERRAULT'S FAIRY TALES, translated by A. E. Johnson and S. R. Littlewood, with 34 full-page illustrations by Gustave Doré. All the original Perrault stories— Cinderella, Sleeping Beauty, Bluebeard, Little Red Riding Hood, Puss in Boots, Tom Thumb, etc.—with their witty verse morals and the magnificent illustrations of Doré. One of the five or six great books of European fairy tales. viii + 117pp. 8⅛ x 11. 22311-6 Paperbound $2.00

OLD HUNGARIAN FAIRY TALES, Baroness Orczy. Favorites translated and adapted by author of the *Scarlet Pimpernel.* Eight fairy tales include "The Suitors of Princess Fire-Fly," "The Twin Hunchbacks," "Mr. Cuttlefish's Love Story," and "The Enchanted Cat." This little volume of magic and adventure will captivate children as it has for generations. 90 drawings by Montagu Barstow. 96pp.
22293-4 Paperbound $1.95

THE RED FAIRY BOOK, Andrew Lang. Lang's color fairy books have long been children's favorites. This volume includes Rapunzel, Jack and the Bean-stalk and 35 other stories, familiar and unfamiliar. 4 plates, 93 illustrations x + 367pp.
21673-X Paperbound $2.50

THE BLUE FAIRY BOOK, Andrew Lang. Lang's tales come from all countries and all times. Here are 37 tales from Grimm, the Arabian Nights, Greek Mythology, and other fascinating sources. 8 plates, 130 illustrations. xi + 390pp.
21437-0 Paperbound $2.50

HOUSEHOLD STORIES BY THE BROTHERS GRIMM. Classic English-language edition of the well-known tales — Rumpelstiltskin, Snow White, Hansel and Gretel, The Twelve Brothers, Faithful John, Rapunzel, Tom Thumb (52 stories in all). Translated into simple, straightforward English by Lucy Crane. Ornamented with headpieces, vignettes, elaborate decorative initials and a dozen full-page illustrations by Walter Crane. x + 269pp.
21080-4 Paperbound **$2.00**

THE MERRY ADVENTURES OF ROBIN HOOD, Howard Pyle. The finest modern versions of the traditional ballads and tales about the great English outlaw. Howard Pyle's complete prose version, with every word, every illustration of the first edition. Do not confuse this facsimile of the original (1883) with modern editions that change text or illustrations. 23 plates plus many page decorations. xxii + 296pp.
22043-5 Paperbound $2.50

THE STORY OF KING ARTHUR AND HIS KNIGHTS, Howard Pyle. The finest children's version of the life of King Arthur; brilliantly retold by Pyle, with 48 of his most imaginative illustrations. xviii + 313pp. 6⅛ x 9¼.
21445-1 Paperbound $2.50

THE WONDERFUL WIZARD OF OZ, L. Frank Baum. America's finest children's book in facsimile of first edition with all Denslow illustrations in full color. The edition a child should have. Introduction by Martin Gardner. 23 color plates, scores of drawings. iv + 267pp.
20691-2 Paperbound $2.50

THE MARVELOUS LAND OF OZ, L. Frank Baum. The second Oz book, every bit as imaginative as the Wizard. The hero is a boy named Tip, but the Scarecrow and the Tin Woodman are back, as is the Oz magic. 16 color plates, 120 drawings by John R. Neill. 287pp.
20692-0 Paperbound $2.50

THE MAGICAL MONARCH OF MO, L. Frank Baum. Remarkable adventures in a land even stranger than Oz. The best of Baum's books not in the Oz series. 15 color plates and dozens of drawings by Frank Verbeck. xviii + 237pp.
21892-9 Paperbound $2.25

THE BAD CHILD'S BOOK OF BEASTS, MORE BEASTS FOR WORSE CHILDREN, A MORAL ALPHABET, Hilaire Belloc. Three complete humor classics in one volume. Be kind to the frog, and do not call him names . . . and 28 other whimsical animals. Familiar favorites and some not so well known. Illustrated by Basil Blackwell. 156pp.
(USO) 20749-8 Paperbound $1.50

EAST O' THE SUN AND WEST O' THE MOON, George W. Dasent. Considered the best of all translations of these Norwegian folk tales, this collection has been enjoyed by generations of children (and folklorists too). Includes True and Untrue, Why the Sea is Salt, East O' the Sun and West O' the Moon, Why the Bear is Stumpy-Tailed, Boots and the Troll, The Cock and the Hen, Rich Peter the Pedlar, and 52 more. The only edition with all 59 tales. 77 illustrations by Erik Werenskiold and Theodor Kittelsen. xv + 418pp.   22521-6 Paperbound $3.50

GOOPS AND HOW TO BE THEM, Gelett Burgess. Classic of tongue-in-cheek humor, masquerading as etiquette book. 87 verses, twice as many cartoons, show mischievous Goops as they demonstrate to children virtues of table manners, neatness, courtesy, etc. Favorite for generations. viii + 88pp. 6½ x 9¼.
22233-0 Paperbound $1.25

ALICE'S ADVENTURES UNDER GROUND, Lewis Carroll. The first version, quite different from the final *Alice in Wonderland,* printed out by Carroll himself with his own illustrations. Complete facsimile of the "million dollar" manuscript Carroll gave to Alice Liddell in 1864. Introduction by Martin Gardner. viii + 96pp. Title and dedication pages in color.   21482-6 Paperbound $1.25

THE BROWNIES, THEIR BOOK, Palmer Cox. Small as mice, cunning as foxes, exuberant and full of mischief, the Brownies go to the zoo, toy shop, seashore, circus, etc., in 24 verse adventures and 266 illustrations. Long a favorite, since their first appearance in St. Nicholas Magazine. xi + 144pp. 6⅝ x 9¼.
21265-3 Paperbound $1.75

SONGS OF CHILDHOOD, Walter De La Mare. Published (under the pseudonym Walter Ramal) when De La Mare was only 29, this charming collection has long been a favorite children's book. A facsimile of the first edition in paper, the 47 poems capture the simplicity of the nursery rhyme and the ballad, including such lyrics as I Met Eve, Tartary, The Silver Penny. vii + 106pp. (USO) 21972-0 Paperbound
$1.25

THE COMPLETE NONSENSE OF EDWARD LEAR, Edward Lear. The finest 19th-century humorist-cartoonist in full: all nonsense limericks, zany alphabets, Owl and Pussycat, songs, nonsense botany, and more than 500 illustrations by Lear himself. Edited by Holbrook Jackson. xxix + 287pp.   (USO) 20167-8 Paperbound $2.00

BILLY WHISKERS: THE AUTOBIOGRAPHY OF A GOAT, Frances Trego Montgomery. A favorite of children since the early 20th century, here are the escapades of that rambunctious, irresistible and mischievous goat—Billy Whiskers. Much in the spirit of *Peck's Bad Boy,* this is a book that children never tire of reading or hearing. All the original familiar illustrations by W. H. Fry are included: 6 color plates, 18 black and white drawings. 159pp.   22345-0 Paperbound $2.00

MOTHER GOOSE MELODIES. Faithful republication of the fabulously rare Munroe and Francis "copyright 1833" Boston edition—the most important Mother Goose collection, usually referred to as the "original." Familiar rhymes plus many rare ones, with wonderful old woodcut illustrations. Edited by E. F. Bleiler. 128pp. 4½ x 6⅜.   22577-1 Paperbound $1.00

CATALOGUE OF DOVER BOOKS

TWO LITTLE SAVAGES; BEING THE ADVENTURES OF TWO BOYS WHO LIVED AS INDIANS AND WHAT THEY LEARNED, Ernest Thompson Seton. Great classic of nature and boyhood provides a vast range of woodlore in most palatable form, a genuinely entertaining story. Two farm boys build a teepee in woods and live in it for a month, working out Indian solutions to living problems, star lore, birds and animals, plants, etc. 293 illustrations. vii + 286pp.

20985-7 Paperbound $2.50

PETER PIPER'S PRACTICAL PRINCIPLES OF PLAIN & PERFECT PRONUNCIATION. Alliterative jingles and tongue-twisters of surprising charm, that made their first appearance in America about 1830. Republished in full with the spirited woodcut illustrations from this earliest American edition. 32pp. 4½ x 6⅜.

22560-7 Paperbound $1.00

SCIENCE EXPERIMENTS AND AMUSEMENTS FOR CHILDREN, Charles Vivian. 73 easy experiments, requiring only materials found at home or easily available, such as candles, coins, steel wool, etc.; illustrate basic phenomena like vacuum, simple chemical reaction, etc. All safe. Modern, well-planned. Formerly *Science Games for Children*. 102 photos, numerous drawings. 96pp. 6⅛ x 9¼.

21856-2 Paperbound $1.25

AN INTRODUCTION TO CHESS MOVES AND TACTICS SIMPLY EXPLAINED, Leonard Barden. Informal intermediate introduction, quite strong in explaining reasons for moves. Covers basic material, tactics, important openings, traps, positional play in middle game, end game. Attempts to isolate patterns and recurrent configurations. Formerly *Chess*. 58 figures. 102pp. (USO) 21210-6 Paperbound $1.25

LASKER'S MANUAL OF CHESS, Dr. Emanuel Lasker. Lasker was not only one of the five great World Champions, he was also one of the ablest expositors, theorists, and analysts. In many ways, his Manual, permeated with his philosophy of battle, filled with keen insights, is one of the greatest works ever written on chess. Filled with analyzed games by the great players. A single-volume library that will profit almost any chess player, beginner or master. 308 diagrams. xli x 349pp.

20640-8 Paperbound $2.75

THE MASTER BOOK OF MATHEMATICAL RECREATIONS, Fred Schuh. In opinion of many the finest work ever prepared on mathematical puzzles, stunts, recreations; exhaustively thorough explanations of mathematics involved, analysis of effects, citation of puzzles and games. Mathematics involved is elementary. Translated bv F. Göbel. 194 figures. xxiv + 430pp. 22134-2 Paperbound $3.50

MATHEMATICS, MAGIC AND MYSTERY, Martin Gardner. Puzzle editor for Scientific American explains mathematics behind various mystifying tricks: card tricks, stage "mind reading," coin and match tricks, counting out games, geometric dissections, etc. Probability sets, theory of numbers clearly explained. Also provides more than 400 tricks, guaranteed to work, that you can do. 135 illustrations. xii + 176pp.

20335-2 Paperbound $1.75

MATHEMATICAL PUZZLES FOR BEGINNERS AND ENTHUSIASTS, Geoffrey Mott-Smith. 189 puzzles from easy to difficult—involving arithmetic, logic, algebra, properties of digits, probability, etc.—for enjoyment and mental stimulus. Explanation of mathematical principles behind the puzzles. 135 illustrations. viii + 248pp.
20198-8 Paperbound $1.75

PAPER FOLDING FOR BEGINNERS, William D. Murray and Francis J. Rigney. Easiest book on the market, clearest instructions on making interesting, beautiful origami. Sail boats, cups, roosters, frogs that move legs, bonbon boxes, standing birds, etc. 40 projects; more than 275 diagrams and photographs. 94pp.
20713-7 Paperbound $1.00

TRICKS AND GAMES ON THE POOL TABLE, Fred Herrmann. 79 tricks and games—some solitaires, some for two or more players, some competitive games—to entertain you between formal games. Mystifying shots and throws, unusual caroms, tricks involving such props as cork, coins, a hat, etc. Formerly *Fun on the Pool Table.* 77 figures. 95pp.
21814-7 Paperbound $1.00

HAND SHADOWS TO BE THROWN UPON THE WALL: A SERIES OF NOVEL AND AMUSING FIGURES FORMED BY THE HAND, Henry Bursill. Delightful picturebook from great-grandfather's day shows how to make 18 different hand shadows: a bird that flies, duck that quacks, dog that wags his tail, camel, goose, deer, boy, turtle, etc. Only book of its sort. vi + 33pp. 6½ x 9¼.   21779-5 Paperbound $1.00

WHITTLING AND WOODCARVING, E. J. Tangerman. 18th printing of best book on market. "If you can cut a potato you can carve" toys and puzzles, chains, chessmen, caricatures, masks, frames, woodcut blocks, surface patterns, much more. Information on tools, woods, techniques. Also goes into serious wood sculpture from Middle Ages to present, East and West. 464 photos, figures. x + 293pp.
20965-2 Paperbound $2.00

HISTORY OF PHILOSOPHY, Julián Marias. Possibly the clearest, most easily followed, best planned, most useful one-volume history of philosophy on the market; neither skimpy nor overfull. Full details on system of every major philosopher and dozens of less important thinkers from pre-Socratics up to Existentialism and later. Strong on many European figures usually omitted. Has gone through dozens of editions in Europe. 1966 edition, translated by Stanley Appelbaum and Clarence Strowbridge. xviii + 505pp.   21739-6 Paperbound $3.50

YOGA: A SCIENTIFIC EVALUATION, Kovoor T. Behanan. Scientific but non-technical study of physiological results of yoga exercises; done under auspices of Yale U. Relations to Indian thought, to psychoanalysis, etc. 16 photos. xxiii + 270pp.
20505-3 Paperbound $2.50

Prices subject to change without notice.
Available at your book dealer or write for free catalogue to Dept. GI, Dover Publications, Inc., 180 Varick St., N. Y., N. Y. 10014. Dover publishes more than 150 books each year on science, elementary and advanced mathematics, biology, music, art, literary history, social sciences and other areas.